A Priest For Ever

A Priest For Ever

a study of typology and
eschatology in Hebrews

Jerome Smith OP

Sheed and Ward · London and Sydney

First published 1969
Sheed and Ward Ltd, 33 Maiden Lane, London WC2, and
Sheed and Ward Pty Ltd, 204 Clarence Road, Sydney NSW 2000

Nihil obstat : C. Kearns OP DSS
           J. Salguero OP DSS
           John M. T. Barton STD LSS Censors

Imprimatur : + Patrick Casey, Vicar General
Westminster, 29 November, 1968

Standard book number : 7220 0557 1
This book is set in 12/14 pt. Linotype Baskerville
Made and printed in Great Britain by
William Clowes and Sons Ltd, London and Beccles

Contents

Contents

1
Introduction

Devotional and theological studies of priesthood abound, filling the bookshelves of clergy-houses and seminaries. In all of them the priesthood of priests within the church is shown to be founded upon the priesthood of Christ, which is set before us in the epistle to the Hebrews. And within the narrower field of New Testament studies the literature on Hebrews is immense, and shows no sign of falling off. Some word of explanation seems in order, saying why I have thought it useful to write yet another book on this subject.

Perhaps an autobiographical approach is as good as any. I have spent the last ten years lecturing in a seminary for African students in South Africa. Here I have been continuously brought up against the caste system of traditional clerical education in a way that was new to me and in a context in which it seemed utterly foreign, in my eyes though not in the students'. Ordination cards are an annual symbol and reminder of this. I am thinking, for the moment, only of the texts and quotations given. Far and away the favourite is the text from Hebrews and Psalm 110: 'Thou art a priest for ever according to the order of Melchizedek'.

This text is, of course, a favourite one in English clerical literature also, and may, for all I know, occur with unthinking regularity on English ordination cards. But it *is* accepted in an unthinking way; few if any ordinands and devotional writers have asked themselves seriously: 'Who is this Melchizedek and what has he to do with me? What is the function and meaning of this Psalm quotation in Hebrews and what light does it throw on the notion of the priesthood of Christ? What then is the relationship between the priesthood of Christ and the priesthood of catholic priests?' The text has a soothing and reassuring effect in spiritual and devotional writing precisely because these questions are not asked; and it is probable that as we read we do instinctively take the reference to Melchizedek as a piece of allegory. We probably do take this text as a poetic equivalent of that other familiar text from Hebrews, which is runner-up to the favourite on ordination cards: 'Every high priest chosen from among men is appointed to act on behalf of men in relation to God, to offer gifts and sacrifices for sins'.

This second text can be read in a straightforward

way as a description of the function of catholic priests, with the minor modification of the omission of the word 'high', and even that can be left in when one is talking of bishops. And yet these two texts do co-exist in Hebrews; and once the strangeness of the Melchizedek text has been felt one has to go on and ask if the second text is not equally strange and foreign, though in a less obvious way. This, at any rate, I found myself compelled to do. Precisely because I was now working in a country where animal sacrifice is part of daily living for the traditional tribesmen, though not for educated urban Africans —I have witnessed one of the initiation sacrifices in the Transkei and shared the meat of the pagan Xhosa tribesmen—the partial and largely unconscious allegorisation of the catholic priesthood and sacramental ritual was brought out into the open in a new way. A fully literal, traditionally catholic acceptance of the ritual character of priesthood and sacrament seems as natural as breathing to the students with whom I work; and yet to the onlooker, though not to them, Melchizedek and all he stands for in Hebrews seems irredeemably foreign.

With these questions in mind I found myself driven back to a direct study of Hebrews: Hebrews is, after all, the only book of the bible to apply the words 'priest' and 'high priest' to Jesus. At an early stage I came across A. Gelin's essay on the priesthood of Christ in Hebrews (in *The sacrament of holy*

1*

orders) which ends with these two sentences: 'The question of our own priesthood does not arise in Hebrews, nor does the eucharist. It can only be with the greatest caution that any conclusions can be drawn about priestly spirituality from this epistle.' This suggests a difference in nature between the priesthood of Christ and that of catholic priests. I have since come to think that that is wrong; but in any case it was clear that any study of the nature of the priesthood of catholic priests would have to be preceded by a study of the priesthood of Christ in Hebrews. That is the theme of this book.

Hebrews must clearly be studied against its context in the early church revealed to us in other New Testament writings. The more one takes note of the astonishing fact that it is only Hebrews that speaks explicitly of the priesthood of Christ the more one is driven to ask what Hebrews means by this. Is the priesthood of Christ in Hebrews a literal concept or is it a piece of biblical symbolism, as many scholars have thought? All the commentators are agreed that both typology and allegory are to be found in Hebrews; what is the limit of these, and how are they inter-related? Typology is often, perhaps invariably, found in connection with eschatology in the bible; how is the typology of Hebrews related to its eschatology, an element which is admittedly of the greatest importance in Hebrews? The replies to these questions will enable one to state the relationship between Old Testament priesthood and Christ's priesthood in Hebrews: is it fundamentally one of continuity or of discontinuity? In answering this question the nature of Christ's priesthood should at last come clear for us.

First of all the present state of opinion about typology, allegory and the various forms of literal statement found in the New Testament generally, and in Hebrews in particular, has been examined. That is the work of chapter 2. I have found the book by James Barr: *Old and New in Interpretation* especially helpful in this matter. My own preliminary conclusion, for which evidence drawn from many different parts of the epistle is presented, is that the priesthood of Christ in Hebrews is a consistent piece of 'allegorical' typology. My notion of 'allegorical' typology is a development of Barr's conception of the use of the Old Testament in the New, in which 'allegory' points to arbitrary elements in the typology.

Chapter 3 sets out to confirm this preliminary conclusion by proving that the 'allegorical' typology of priesthood in Hebrews is consistent throughout the epistle, and not a mere occasional flourish found in some sections. Here the study of the literary structure of Hebrews carried out by Albert Vanhoye is an essential part of my argument. Vanhoye's brilliant work is exhaustive and rather exhausting to read; it is enough for the purpose of this book to

select only a part of his analysis, sufficient to mark
off the different sections of Hebrews and to show
their essential interdependence. The other half of
the argument of the chapter is to point to the 'allegorical' elements in the priesthood typology as it is
gradually unfolded in the epistle from first chapter
to last. This demonstration of the unified literary
structure and of the consistent 'allegorical' typology
demands a considerable amount of close textual
work: I must ask for the reader's patience and for-
bearance as this part of the argument unfolds.

Once the consistent 'allegorical' typology is
proven, we are ready to approach the eschatology of
Hebrews. Even though priesthood in the literal
sense is a sacred social function and office, an 'allegorical' priesthood is not a social office, and therefore
the 'allegorical' priesthood of Christ can, and does,
stand at an infinite, indeed precisely eschatological,
distance from the Old Testament priesthoods. In
the language of Hebrews: 'if he were on earth, he
would not be a priest at all, since there are priests
who offer gifts according to the law' (8:4). In the fact
that Christ stands outside the historical and social
succession of the Old Testament priesthood his
unique eschatological role can be clearly seen. It is
because Christ 'offered' himself through the eternal
Spirit (9:14), that he stands right outside, and brings
to an end once for all the earthly, historical, priestly
succession. The fourth chapter of this book is directly

concerned with this 'realised' eschatology of Hebrews
and with its relationship to the 'allegorical' typology
of priesthood. It is argued that only the typological
reading of Hebrews can allow the eschatology to
come through with its full and definitive force.

The body of the book, therefore, is concerned
only with Hebrews. Another book would be needed
to trace and evaluate the sacrificial and priestly
motifs occurring elsewhere in the New Testament.
But consciously or unconsciously the 'priestly' interpretation of Christ's work in Hebrews has pro-
foundly affected studies of these motifs in the rest
of the New Testament. This is explicitly acknowledged in Markus Barth's recent fine study *Was
Christ's death a sacrifice?* I thought it useful, therefore, in my concluding chapter, to try and draw
some conclusions from my study of Hebrews in relation to these other New Testament motifs. This I
have done by attempting to show that there are very
serious gaps in Barth's argument. I leave it to the
reader to judge how far I have been successful in
this. It does, perhaps, at least appear that any reassessment of Christ's priesthood in Hebrews will
call for a re-examination of our interpretations of
the other New Testament affirmations about the
sacrifice of Christ. My own guess is that the fundamental discontinuity between Christ's priesthood
and Old Testament priesthood in Hebrews will be
paralleled by a fundamental discontinuity between

Old and New Testament sacrifice, and therefore priesthood, in other New Testament writings.

The Greek text I have used is that edited by K. Aland, M. Black, B. M. Metzger and A. Wikgren for the American and various other Bible Societies in 1966. For the English translation I have used the Revised Standard Version. Any modifications, or preferences of the footnote rendering over that in the text (Vanhoye has shown that eg, the omission of the name 'Christ' at 10:5 and 10:12, reported in RSV footnote, has a structural significance in the composition of the chapter) have been noted as they occur.

This dissertation was written under the direction of the Very Revd Fr Kearns OP. In spite of his many administrative and scholarly preoccupations he has made time to guide and help me in the writing of this essay. I am very grateful to him for his unfailing patience and kindness.

2
General considerations on typology and eschatology in Hebrews

To read the epistle to the Hebrews is to enter gradually into a strange world: the familiar themes of the culmination of prophecy, and the typologies of Moses and Christ, Israel and the church, are gradually left behind, and the familiar Jesus of the gospels is transmuted into a remote high-priestly figure who purifies 'the heavenly things' (Heb 9:23), whatever they may be, with better bloody sacrifices than those of Old Testament ritual. Hebrews stands apart from the rest of the New Testament in so far as here only do we find Jesus spoken of in priestly and high-priestly language. 1 Corinthians and the synoptic gospels report a sacrificial saying of Jesus over the 'cup of blessing' at the last supper, the fourth gospel presents Jesus as using the words that are perhaps implicitly sacrificial in his post-supper discourse, but only in Hebrews do we find the words 'priest' and 'high-priest' applied to Jesus.

I will return briefly to the question of possible sources for the great theme of the priesthood of Jesus in Hebrews, the 'main point' (8:1) of the whole epistle, in the conclusion to this essay. My main purpose is rather to examine the nature of priesthood in Hebrews, and to ask how it is related to that other most important theme, on which Hebrews places a quite special emphasis, the unique, definitive, eschatological realisation of God's saving work in Christ.

Opinions differ very widely as to the nature of Christ's priesthood in Hebrews, from those who take it absolutely literally to those who think of it as an allegory or extended metaphor. There is very wide agreement that Hebrews contains typology, a substantial number of scholars recognise allegorical elements in it, but there is a bewildering variety of theories as to what constitutes a typology or an allegory, and how they are related to one another. One writer sees the priesthood of Christ and the Old Testament in terms of the classical thomist theory of analogy: rejecting metaphor he finds a literal philosophico-theological double analogy in Hebrews. A considerable number of catholic writers appeal to the theory of the *sensus plenior*, the fuller sense, of the Old Testament passages made use of in Hebrews. But even among this group there is disagreement: for some the fuller sense is founded upon a typology of Old Testament realities, for others it is a question of the meaning of Old Testament words.

It is obviously possible to combine these elements in varying ways, and one has the impression that most of the logical possibilities have been upheld by one author or another. It is one thing to recognise the presence of typology, or even allegory, within Hebrews; it is quite another to assess the epistle as a whole as an extended typology or allegory. The fundamental difference in evaluation seems to lie between those who take Christ's priesthood, in Hebrews' conception of it, as a literal priesthood, while possibly admitting a secondary usage of allegory and metaphor, and those who see it as an extended metaphor. Typology is ambiguous, it can be assessed as literal or as metaphorical. It is possible therefore to arrange the different theories on a sliding scale from the literal to the metaphorical: the genus and species theory, the strict analogy, the *sensus plenior*, the typology, and finally the allegory theory.

The upholder of the genus and species theory is C. Spicq. This is combined with the discernment of allegorical exegesis in 7 : 3, and of a typological relationship between Melchizedek and Christ, as also between the levitical priesthood and Christ. Here is the passage in which Spicq puts forward his theory:

Whatever divergences and oppositions there may be between the old and the new priesthoods, Hebrews could not, without destroying the whole proof-value of its thesis, bring in a new definition of the priestly institution to be applied to Christ alone. The confrontation makes no sense save in terms of a fundamental likeness. The Melchizedek priesthood and the levitical priesthood are like two species of a single genus which contain in their own way the essential elements of every kind of *hierosunē;* it is only on this basis that they can be compared, after the same fashion as the old and the new *diathēkē*. Though the one does not attain to *teleiōsis* (7 : 11) while the other is *aparabaton* (7 : 24), this is only a change of quality within the one institution; though it is of such great importance that it brings about the change from one covenant to the other (7 : 12).[1]

The Melchizedek priesthood is, in the context, the priesthood of Christ. Though Spicq inserts a saving 'like' (*comme*) before the 'two species', the context demands that he is speaking literally.

This view seems to rest upon a doubtful assessment of Hebrews as an apologetic. It is rather a 'word of exhortation' (13 : 22) in which, as in all good sermons, there is a strong doctrinal element, and new points of doctrine have to be established and supported.[2] I would agree with those scholars,

---

[1] C. Spicq, *L'Epître aux Hébreux* II, Paris 1952–53, 126 (2 vols).
[2] Cf J. Van Der Ploeg, 'L'exégèse de l'Ancien Testament dans l'Epître aux Hébreux', in *Revue Biblique* LIV (1947), 227: '... I

eg A. Vanhoye,[3] who see the idea of Christ's priesthood as just such a piece of new teaching (against
Spicq), and therefore the argumentative element,
though secondary, is of particular importance in
Hebrews: this does not suffice to turn it into an
apologetic.

More seriously still, Spicq's rejection of a new
institution and a new definition, and *a fortiori* of
an allegorical-typological relationship between the
levitical priesthood and Christ's priesthood rests
quite patently on the demand for a proof that would
be convincing to Spicq himself. There can be no
doubt at all, as a comparison of rabbinical and New
Testament methods of scriptural proof will show,
that the New Testament writers, like the rabbis,
found cogent arguments in (to us) quite arbitrary
and 'allegorical' interpretations of Old Testament
texts. Our concern in exegesis of Hebrews is not
with what will suffice to convince ourselves in the
line of the argument from prophecy, fuller sense,
typology, or whatever, but with what the author of
Hebrews accepted by way of scriptural proof.

Further, this attempt to bring Christ's priesthood

---

believe that the author is not an apologist, he does not defend,
rather he expounds and exhorts, and this seems to me very important for a proper understanding of his exegesis. He quotes
from the Old Testament in order to prove something, or to edify,
or sometimes to serve as a vehicle for his own ideas.'

[3] *La structure littéraire de l'Epître aux Hébreux,* Paris 1963,
113.

within the same univocal concept with the levitical priesthood makes it quite impossible to give the 'realised eschatology' of Hebrews its full weight. Minor or major divergences and oppositions may be allowed for within the reach of a genus, but the uniqueness, the definitiveness, the once-for-all (*ephapax*) character of Christ's saving work is fatally compromised by forcing it into the same institution with the levitical priesthood. D. Bertetto has, more plausibly, tried to show that the various forms of priesthood that he discerns in the bible constitute a philosophico-theological analogy.[4] He begins his article by noting that theologians (that is, for Bertetto, catholic theologians) are not yet agreed on the nature and constitutive elements of priesthood and sacrifice. This he attributes to the fact that these theologians have constructed a generic concept of priesthood, either in a purely speculative way or on the basis of natural extra-biblical religions. He rightly urges that we should turn our attention rather to the bible and base ourselves on the notion of priesthood to be found there.

He does not in fact attempt a description of the Old Testament priesthoods, with their varying evolutions through the vicissitudes of the history of the Hebrew people, he goes instead directly to Heb

[4] D. Bertetto, 'La natura del sacerdozio secondo Ebrei 5, 1–4 e le sue realizzazioni nel Nuovo Testamento', *Salesianum* XXVI (1964), 395–440.

5 : 1–4, in which he finds a biblical definition that covers all forms of divinely appointed biblical priesthood. This definition is made up out of four essential elements: a priest must be taken from among men, called by God, consecrated, and exercise a sacrificial mediatorship.

Bertetto then turns to the scholastic theory of analogy. As he correctly remarks, thomists are not in agreement among themselves in their interpretations of St Thomas or in their own constructed theories. He prefers to follow the theory of Cajetan, the classical commentator on Aquinas of the early reformation period, revived in this century by thomists like Penido.[5] It runs as follows: words (*nomina*, but this does not apply only to nouns) are used univocally, where they carry exactly the same meaning, as in generic and specific names; purely equivocally, where it is merely accidental that the same word is used; and analogically, where the meaning is partly the same and partly different. This can happen in two ways: first, where several things are related to one, as when we speak of a healthy man, a healthy diet and a healthy complexion, where only the man is simply speaking healthy, while the diet is a cause of his healthiness and his complexion a sign of it; secondly, where two things are related to two further things in such a way that we may compare the rela-

[5] M. T.-L. Penido, *Le rôle de l'analogie en théologie dogmatique*, Paris 1931.

tionships or *proportiones*. This may be done through transference, improperly, and that is metaphor, or it may be done directly and properly, when the relational concept, or better the reality corresponding to it, belongs inherently and intrinsically in each subject. The first kind of analogy is called, technically, analogy of attribution, the second analogy of proportionality.

Bertetto finds both these kinds of analogy relevant to priesthood in the biblical sense. Christ is priest in an eminent and transcendent way, the mosaic priesthood by an essential relationship of prefiguration and typology (we can leave aside, for present purposes, the other forms of New Testament priesthood of which Bertetto speaks): this establishes an analogy of attribution. Further, the four essential elements of priesthood are found intrinsically, in a way proportionate to their place in God's plan, both in Christ and in the mosaic priesthood: this sets up an analogy of proportionality.

This theory seems vulnerable to criticism on two main counts: the idea of priesthood is only superficially drawn from Hebrews, it is still an abstract theological notion torn from its living context there; and, secondly, it appears to rest upon the mistaken idea that typology can, as it is actually used in the New Testament generally and in Hebrews in particular, be successfully disentangled from allegory and from related, and perhaps to us rather arbitrary, methods of using the Old Testament, as we shall see later.

The literary structure of Hebrews is a subtly and tightly woven one, as Vanhoye has brilliantly demonstrated in his book on the subject. There is a closely patterned relationship of paragraph to paragraph, larger section to larger section, and main part to main part. Heb 5 : 1–4 cannot be understood as the author understood it unless it is seen against the immediate context and the larger context. When, in the next chapter, I attempt to describe the picture of Christ in Hebrews, it will be necessary to show how the literary structure goes to build up the idea; for present purposes some remarks on 4 : 15–5 : 10 will suffice.

These verses, according to Vanhoye, are a section, announced already in 2 : 17–18, on the merciful and compassionate high priest. There are three paragraphs: an introduction, 3 : 15–16, which states the theme in an exhortatory way; 5 : 1–4, which gives a definition of high priesthood; and 5 : 5–10, which applies it to Christ. Heb 5 : 1–4 and 5–10 are particularly closely related, as indeed Bertetto saw, but 5–10 are tied in with the whole central part of the epistle, which runs from 5 : 11 to 10 : 39, since 5 : 9–10 are the formal announcement of the themes of this part. How Jesus is designated by God as a high priest after the order of Melchizedek is explained in chapter 7 in which most commentators find some elements of allegory; how Jesus is made perfect and exercises a more excellent ministry is set forth in chapters 8 and 9 and finally how Jesus is the source of eternal salvation is expounded in 10 : 1–18. In Bertetto's exposition there is a detectable tendency to allow 5 : 1–4, which apparently provide a neat theological definition, to predominate over 5 : 5–10. Vanhoye remarks that we are faced with complementarity, rather than identity between these two sections; this complementarity, which leaves place for infinite difference, can only be properly understood in terms of the epistle as a whole.

Turning now to the theory of the *sensus plenior*, two different varieties are to be found. One is upheld by Spicq, an indication in itself that the theory is an attempt to save the literal historical meaning of the Old Testament in its exploitation by the New. Spicq would prefer to use the phrase 'christological parable' (*parabolisme christologique*), following the language of Heb 9 : 8 where the division of the tent of the desert time and the law that the inner sanctuary, the holy of holies, was to be entered only once a year and only by the high priest, are said to be a parable for the present age. But he explicitly states that his christological parable is identical with the fuller sense of other writers. In this he is mistaken: the fuller sense is normally taken to be the sense of the words of Old Testament passages hidden from the human writer yet intended by God as part of the literal meaning of the text.[6] But for Spicq the fuller sense means that 'beyond the obvious, or rather immediate, meaning of the words the realities that are spoken of are in turn expressive of New Testament (*chrétienne*) realities'. This comes very near to Thomas Aquinas' classical definition of what the fathers and the mediaevals meant by their spiritual or typical senses, but Spicq insists that it is not even an expansion of the literal sense, let alone a multiplication of its meaning, it is a literal, authentic prolongation of the word of God.[7]

Since for Spicq the fuller sense goes through the realities spoken of, its range is immense, it covers the whole of Old Testament worship, priesthood and sacrifice. For other writers, who think of the fuller sense of Old Testament words as referring directly to New Testament realities, the range of the *sensus plenior* in Hebrews is naturally restricted to explicit and implicit quotations from the Old Testament. The explicit quotations have been carefully examined by J. Van Der Ploeg,[8] in an article based throughout on the conception of the *sensus*

[6] The fullest account of the *sensus plenior* is to be found in J. Coppens, *Les harmonies des deux Testaments*, Paris 1949. The abundant literature of the subject has been surveyed by R. E. Brown in two articles in the *Catholic Biblical Quarterly*, 'The history and development of a theory of a *sensus plenior*' in xv (1953), 141–162; 'The *sensus plenior* in the last ten years' in xxv (1963), 252–285.

[7] C. Spicq, I, 348.

[8] *Art cit* in note 2.

plenior. He shows some embarrassment in dealing with the basic proof-text for Christ's priesthood in Hebrews, 'Thou art a priest for ever, after the order of Melchizedek', and does not, indeed, as he does for most of the others, state that the application to Christ is a *sensus plenior* of the psalmist's words; but the general tenor of the article and the explicit affirmation in the conclusion seem to show that this is what Van Der Ploeg has in mind:

> It is the *sensus plenior*, *profundior* that interests him most, a sense sometimes combined with the typological sense. It plays a major role in his exegesis of those texts that do not refer directly and clearly to Christ and to the new economy. The *sensus plenior* is based upon the God-willed harmony of the two testaments, which are related the one to the other as the imperfect to the perfect.[9]

Since the words of Ps 110:4 are vital to the argument of Hebrews, even a more restricted theory of the fuller sense, like that of Van Der Ploeg, leads into the heart of the epistle's meaning.

It emerges very clearly from a reading of Van Der Ploeg's article that the theory of the fuller sense does not arise directly out of the text of Hebrews, for him or for other writers, but is the application to Hebrews of a general theory fashioned in order to 'save the appearances' of the whole New Testa-

[9] *Op cit*, 228.

ment exploitation of the Old. A clear sign of this is the mis-interpretation, by Van Der Ploeg and others, of the idea of perfection (*teleiōsis*) in Hebrews. So pervasive is this mis-interpretation that one expects to find in *teleiōsis* one of the key time-words expressive of the realised eschatology of Hebrews, a word that signifies the once-for-all fulfilment of the Old Testament in the New. A careful examination of all the occurrences of this and other words derived from the same root will reveal that while this is indeed an important conception in Hebrews it never refers to a perfecting of the Old Testament in the New. It belongs indeed to the conception of Christ's priesthood and priestly work: he is made perfect through suffering (5 : 8–9); while the law can never, by the same sacrifices which are offered year after year, make perfect the participants (10 : 1), Christ, by a single offering, has perfected for all time those who are sanctified (10 : 14). But it is never stated that Christ perfects the Old Testament or its institutions. For Van Der Ploeg, however:

> The epistle to the Hebrews contrasts the two economies, that of the Old and that of the New Testament, rather than two worlds; this contrast is conceived of after the fashion of the contrast between the beginning of a movement and its end. The end is the perfection, the *teleiōsis* (7 : 11) towards which the whole old economy moves.[10]

[10] *Op cit*, 189.

To refute this exegesis it is sufficient simply to read the text of 7 : 11: 'Now if perfection had been attainable through the Levitical priesthood (for under it the people received the law), what further need would there have been for another priest to arise after the order of Melchizedek, rather than one named after the order of Aaron?' Quite evidently, it is people, not the law or the levitical priesthood, that are perfected.

The general theory of the *sensus plenior* has been very acutely criticised by Bruce Vawter in an article in the *Catholic Biblical Quarterly*.[11] He points out that supporters of this theory do not sufficiently distinguish between the prophetic (for the moment, and in this context, fore-telling rather than forth-telling) element in the Old Testament and that which goes under the name of the *sensus plenior*. I would agree with that, though an appeal to prophecy will not solve all the difficulties. I shall deal with this more fully when I come to speak of allegory; for the moment it is sufficient to note that Hebrews reads as prophecy texts that were not originally prophetic at all (Ps 40:6–8 in Heb 10:5–7), and transfers prophetic texts to a quite new context (Jer 31:31–34 in Heb 8:8–12).

Vawter's main criticism is that the *sensus plenior* theory endangers, without sufficient reason given,

---

[11] B. Vawter, 'The fuller sense, some considerations', in xxvi (1964), 85–96.

the whole achievement of critical historical Old Testament scholarship over these last two centuries. We have, most painfully and despite most serious difficulties and prejudices, come to recover something of the real meaning of Old Testament passages as they were written (or spoken) and according to that very different historical situation (situations) in which they were written (and spoken). The introduction of a further, novel, literal sense necessarily endangers the first, immediate (whatever you will) historical sense, the meaning of the human words as they were written (or spoken) by their human authors. We may take it for granted that God knows everything, and therefore all the uses to which biblical words will be put, but how can we possibly allow the divine foreknowledge to prejudice the meaning of divinely inspired words as he inspired them to be written (or spoken)? And theoretically, at least, there is no conceivable, controllable limitation on the meanings that may be read out of Old Testament writings. Though the real, albeit unconfessed, point of the *sensus plenior* theory is to save the New Testament appearances of the Old, the formal theory contains no limitation whatever. We are, once we adopt this theory, and despite our best intentions, fatally caught up into the allegorical fantasies of the fathers and mediaeval (and, for that matter, later) preachers. To quote a passage from Vawter's slightly cryptic conclusion:

The fuller literal sense, it seems to me, can be viewed as a contemporary residue of the Fathers' solution. If, as Benoit concedes, the 'anagogical sense has been rendered superfluous by a better comprehension of the significance of biblical eschatology, we may have cause to believe that the continued re-examination of the word of God will succeed in reducing rather than increasing the number of scriptural 'senses'.[12]

If this means, as I think it does, that we may in any passage, whether of Old Testament, New Testament, fathers or later authors, look to the immediate literal meaning (and by literal I do, of course, mean literary, and literary meaning is often involved in ambiguity and multiplicity: see, for example, W. Empson's *Seven types of ambiguity*, 3rd ed, London 1953) which does very often include the quotation and exploitation, implicit or explicit, of earlier writers, then I am in complete agreement. We do not need any theory of *sensus plenior*, typology, allegory nor even, for the most part, prophecy for our own practice: what we really need to know is how the later stages of the Old Testament interpreted the earlier, how the various New Testament writings understood the Old, and so on. But this brings us to the very delicate question of the relationship between typology and allegory.

[12] Vawter, *op cit*, 96.

Although the word 'typology' does not seem to have existed before the nineteenth century[13] St Paul tells us that Adam was a type of the one who was to come, ie Christ, on one common interpretation of the verse (Rm 5:14). And in 1 Cor 10:11 he says, of the events of the exodus, that these things happened to them *tupikōs*, since they were written down for the instruction of christians. In Hebrews the tent of the desert is called the copy (*hupodeigma*) and shadow (8:5) and *antitupa* (9:24) of heaven and the heavenly sanctuary. Again the word 'allegory' is not used in the New Testament, though it existed in first-century Greek; we do find the verb *allēgoreō* in Gal 4:24, referring to the allegory of Sarah and Hagar, the Old and New covenants and so on.

In the patristic period typology and allegory underwent a tremendous development and extension; few passages of the bible escaped interpretation in this way. The Alexandrian fathers were particularly fond of it, and this provoked a reaction from the Antiochenes, who reproached them, inaccurately, with neglecting the literal sense and with adopting, and in this they were more accurate, pagan Greek methods of allegorising. The Antiochenes tended to avoid describing their own non-literal kinds of

[13] H. De Lubac, ' "Typologie" et "Allégorisme" ', *Recherches de Science Religieuse* XXXIV (1947), 181. *The Shorter Oxford Dictionary* gives 1845 for the English word.

interpretation as allegory,[14] and preferred to speak of 'types'. Chrysostom goes so far as to say that St Paul uses the word 'allegorising' improperly in place of 'type' in Galatians.[15] But it does not seem that St Paul made any distinction between typical and allegorical; and even those modern scholars who share the Antiochene suspicion of allegory and acceptance of typology have to admit that the Antiochenes did fall into allegorical methods of interpretation.[16]

The Antiochenes were an exception among the fathers,[17] and in the middle ages the allegorical sense was either identical with the typical, or spiritual, sense, or was taken to be a branch of it.[18] But the distinction, and the preference for typology, have been revived in modern times. In his article *allēgoreō* in TWNT, Fr Büchsel referred to various attempts[19] that had been made to distinguish between Alexandrian Jewish allegory, that was indifferent to history, and Palestinian Jewish typology, that held to it firmly. Büchsel points out that Philo Judaeus the Alexandrian held firmly to history, and that the Palestinian

[14] K. J. Woollcombe, 'The Biblical origins and patristic development of typology', in *Essays in typology*, London 1957, 57, n 1.

[15] PG 61, col 662. Both De Lubac and Woollcombe refer to this passage.

[16] Woollcombe, *op cit*, 60.

[17] H. De Lubac, *art cit*.

[18] H. De Lubac, *Exégèse Médiévale*, Paris 1959–64 (4 vols).

[19] He refers to the *Jewish Encyclopedia* II, 338, and to O. Michel, *Paulus und Seine Bibel* (1929), 110.

rabbis who rejected Greek allegory are sometimes to be found using similar methods: a difference of degree, not of substance.

In spite of Büchsel's criticism, which might have served as a warning to New Testament and patristic scholars both, the firm (and arbitrary) distinction between typology and allegory, and the preference for typology, are extraordinarily pervasive. J. Daniélou is a most energetic defender both of the distinction and the preference,[20] and harshly criticises De Lubac for not making it.[21] De Lubac somewhat wearily replies that he has never denied the distinction, is not the mere title of his article a proof of that?[22] but points out that (leaving aside the Antiochenes) the fathers and the mediaevals do not make the distinction, which in Daniélou's handling, is too crude, and that their preferred word for what Daniélou likes to call typology is in fact 'allegory'.

This is by no means an argument confined to catholic circles. It turns up with alarming frequency in commentaries upon Hebrews: eg Westcott,[23]

[20] See, for example, Daniélou's *Sacramentum futuri* (translated as *From shadows to reality*, London 1960), and his *Origen*, London 1955.

[21] In his article 'Origène', in the *Supplément au Dictionnaire de la Bible* VI, col 8992.

[22] *Exégèse Médiévale*, 2e Partie, II, 130.

[23] B. F. Westcott, *The Epistle to the Hebrews*, London 1914, 3rd ed, 202. Westcott's distinction between the typical and the allegorical, the one resting upon a real and historical correspondence, the other on points arbitrarily taken, is particularly interesting because of its early date.

Héring,[24] Bruce,[25] and predictably in Dr Lampe's essay 'The reasonableness of typology'.[26] The Daniélou line has been refined and presented most persuasively, perhaps, as a general theory, by R. P. C. Hanson in his book *Allegory and event*,[27] which is concerned particularly with Origen, but contains a chapter devoted to the New Testament, and provides an especially clear statement of the distinction that has struck this school of writers. 'Typology', Hanson declares, 'is the interpreting of an event belonging to the present or the recent past as the fulfilment of a similar situation recorded or prophesied in Scripture'; while 'allegory is the interpretation of an object or person or a number of objects or persons as in reality meaning some object or person of a later time, with no attempt to trace a relationship of "similar situations" between them'.[28]

It is clear that the words 'similar situation' in that quotation have a special meaning for Hanson. St Paul in Gal 4 has surely been struck by a similarity between the situation of Hagar and Sarah and the synagogue (the present Jerusalem) and the church (the Jerusalem above, our mother). What Hanson

[24] J. Héring, *L'Epître aux Hébreux*, Paris 1954, 66, 68.

[25] F. F. Bruce, *Commentary on the Epistle to the Hebrews*, London 1964, l–li.

[26] In *Essays in typology*, 29f. On p 34 he calls 7:3 of Hebrews 'a piece of sheer allegorizing'.

[27] London 1959.

[28] *Op cit*, 7.

really means is surely that some similarities strike him as convincing, and these he calls typologies, others do not, and those he calls allegories. The distinction rests upon a particular view of history, and a very high value set upon what is thought to be the true biblical view of history; unfortunately, St Paul does not seem altogether to share it.

This whole modern attitude to history and biblical history has been subjected to a close and critical examination by J. Barr, in his book *Old and New in Interpretation*.[29] He points out many difficulties both in the theories about the true biblical view of history and the way in which these theories underlie the distinction between typology and allegory and the preference for typology. My criticism of Hanson above is an application of Barr's general line of criticism to Hanson's particular case. Barr holds that no watertight distinction can be made, and that the rejection of allegory cannot be founded upon the New Testament. He goes on to point out that, in any case, typology and allegory need to be brought into relationship with other New Testament ways of using the Old.

Thus we can easily list as many as seven kinds of situation:

(a) explicit types, eg Moses and Christ
(b) real allegory, eg the muzzled ox

[29] London 1966. The quotation is from p 115.

   (c) paraenesis, eg Balaam, Sarah
   (d) fulfilments of prophecies cited
   (e) proofs from linguistic details, eg 'seeds'
   (f) situation similarities in style and language, e.g. the Magnificat
   (g) situation similarities in action.

As will readily be understood, even this classification is artificial, in that these uses may be mixed up, and passage is easily made from one to another.

To Barr's list I should like to add:

   (h) the transference of prophecy
   (i) the taking as prophecy of non-prophetical texts
   (j) the changing or cutting short of texts
   (k) the tailoring of implicit quotations to fill in with later ideas.

I think that most of these, or something very like them, are to be found in Hebrews. This needs detailed substantiation, since this is an important part of the evidence upon which my theory that the priesthood of Christ in Hebrews is a sustained 'allegorical' typology rests. (By 'allegorical' I wish to include procedures (b) to (k) above.)

   (a) It is agreed by all commentators that there are types in Hebrews. The Moses–Christ typology is found in 3 : 1–6. Melchizedek, whatever allegorical elements there may be, is clearly a type of Christ. And since Aaron makes a discreet appearance as high priest in 5 : 4 (cf 9 : 4), it is clear that there is a typological relationship in the high priest–Christ parallel. There are a number of typologies in chapter 11, eg Isaac (11 : 19), and again Moses (11 : 23–28).

(b) Barr's example, the muzzled ox, seems to indicate that by 'real allegory' he means a use of an Old Testament text in which the literal, historical meaning, as modern scholarship would establish this, is explicitly denied. It is not obvious, at first sight, that there is anything like this in Hebrews, but I would suggest that something like it is involved in Hebrews' contention, in 9 : 9–10 and elsewhere, that the Old Testament sacrifices for sin, and in particular the sacrifices of the day of atonement, had a ritual effect only and could not effect any change in relationship to God. Hebrews' idea has obvious affinities with Paul's evaluation of the law, and those who agree with them in their evaluations, and hold that this is not an expression of the new situation brought in by Christ, but a true judgment on the past in its pastness, will obviously not agree. For myself, I should like to make my own an observation of J. Cambier: 'despite what Hebrews says about them, the old sacrifices were acceptable to God and useful to those

who offered them'.[30] No doubt they were so in virtue
of the power of Christ's passion and exaltation; if it
is maintained that they were not it is difficult to see
how Leviticus, to go no further, was ever in any real
sense a word of God. Hebrews, in denying the moral
efficacy of Old Testament sacrifice denies their real
truth as sacrifices, and at the same time regards them
as prefigurations of the sacrifice of Christ (9:12):
that is a piece of 'real allegory'.

(c) Since Hebrews is as a whole a word of exhortation it is naturally well supplied with paraenetical
examples from the Old Testament. For warning examples one may take the fathers of the desert time
(3:7-4, 11); for encouraging examples Gideon,
Barak and the others in 11:32-40.

(d) The theme of the fulfilment of prophecy is
certainly an important one in Hebrews. Since, however, I have added to Barr's list three further kinds
of use: the transference of prophecy, the taking as
prophecy of non-prophetical texts, and the changing
or cutting short of texts (some of which may be prophetical or taken by Hebrews to be so) the situation
becomes more complicated. The two proof-texts in
5:5-6 are sometimes taken as both prophetical and
as a foretelling of Christ: but this is usually done
through an appeal to the *sensus plenior* or to the
messianic re-reading of these texts in later judaism.

[30] 'Eschatologie ou hellénisme dans l'Epître aux Hébreux',
Salesianum II (1949), 71, n 76.

The prophecy with the best credentials for a plain 'fulfilment of prophecy cited' is probably the prophecy from Jeremiah about the new covenant. I should prefer to class this with transferred prophecies, and shall indicate briefly why.

Jer 31 : 31–34 has not passed with its authenticity unquestioned, but the reason generally advanced, that Jeremiah was a prophet of woe, not of salvation, can hardly stand. Few scholars would wish to challenge the authenticity of Jeremiah's action in buying the ancestral family field at Anathoth, nor of his accompanying prophecy: 'thus says the Lord of hosts, the God of Israel: Houses and fields and vineyards shall again be bought in this land'. The question of authenticity is in any case a secondary one, the prophecy of the new covenant belongs, whether it is Jeremiah's or not, with the other prophecies of restoration that occur from the letter of Jeremiah in chapter 29 onwards. Jer 29 : 10–11 runs: 'For thus says the Lord: When seventy years are completed for Babylon, I will visit you, and I will fulfil to you my promise and bring you back to this place. For I know the plans I have for you, says the Lord, plans for welfare and not for evil, to give you a future and a hope.' The theme of return and restoration runs all through chapter 30. Chapter 31 itself begins: 'At that time says the Lord, I will be the God of all the families of Israel, and they shall be my people. Thus says the Lord: the people who survived the sword found grace in the wilderness . . . I have loved you with an everlasting love; therefore I have continued my faithfulness to you. Again I will build you, and you shall be built, O virgin Israel!' Chapter 32, which tells the story of the buying of the field, has a long prophecy, said to have been spoken by Jeremiah on that occasion, which contains another saying about covenant:

> Now therefore thus says the Lord, the God of Israel: Behold, I will gather them from all the countries to which I drove them in my anger and my wrath and in great indignation; I will bring them back to this place, and I will make them dwell in safety. And they shall be my people, and I will be their God. I will give them one heart and one way, that they may fear me for ever, for their own good and the good of their children after them. I will make with them an everlasting covenant, that I will not turn away from doing good to them; and I will put the fear of me in their hearts, that they may not turn from me. I will rejoice in doing them good, and I will plant them in this land in faithfulness, with all my heart and with all my soul.

On the basis of this evidence from the wider context, I think it has to be admitted that Jeremiah was speaking of a return, a restoration, and a new covenant, an everlasting covenant in the near future ('seventy years'—of course a round figure). If we are to look for a direct, literal, though admittedly dis-appointing, fulfilment of Jeremiah's prophecy we have to turn to the covenant-making activities de-scribed in the books of Ezra (10 : 3) and Nehemiah (9 : 38), or perhaps to earlier ones of the time of the return that have gone unrecorded.

A. Vanhoye, with his usual acuity, has seen that Jeremiah's prophecy of the new covenant does not apply in any direct, simple way to the covenant of the last supper: he thinks of Jeremiah's covenant as a simple renewal of the Sinai covenant, rather than as a radically new covenant. His ground, though, is a rather curious one: it is in the absence of any mention of a new sacrifice that he finds reason to deny any conception of a really new covenant.[30a] There is certainly no mention of sacrifice in Jer 31 : 31–34, but 34 : 8ff speaks of a covenant and a sacrifice. The covenant is quite explicitly a renewal of the Sinai covenant (34 : 13), with special emphasis on one of the regulations of the Sinai covenant, at least as this is presented in Exodus, whatever the historical pro-venance of the regulation (Ex 21 : 2 and Jer 34 : 14). Given that covenant renewal could, even at so late a date, carry with it a renewal of covenant sacrifice, one may reasonably ask whether the passover sacri-fice of 2 Kgs 23 was not intended by Josiah and the people as a covenant sacrifice ('For no such passover

[30a] 'De instauratione novae dispensationis' Heb 9 : 15–23, *Verbum Domini*, XLIV (1966), 115.

2*

had been kept since the days of the judges who judged Israel, or during all the days of the kings of Israel or of the kings of Judah; but in the eighteenth year of King Josiah this passover was kept to the Lord in Jerusalem' (23:22–23)). This opens up the possibility that there were covenant sacrifices in Moab (Dt 29:1) and Shechem (Jos 24), even though sacrifices are not explicitly mentioned there, perhaps in order to bring out the significance of Sinai as the place of *the* covenant and *the* covenant sacrifice. In any case it seems questionable, in view of Jer 34, whether the novelty of the new covenant can be made to depend upon a new sacrifice; a novel sacrifice, such as we find in the New Testament, does introduce a novel covenant. Vanhoye's exegesis is thus, and so far, vindicated; his sense of the gap between Jer 31 and the last supper in the pauline, and possibly Hebrews', version (Heb 9:20), seems well founded. For this reason I prefer to leave Barr's category (d) untenanted in Hebrews.

(e) Barr's example of a proof from linguistic details, 'seeds', is of course a reference to Paul's argument in Gal 3:16 that the promise made to Abraham and his seed in Gn 12:7 refers to Christ since the word 'seed' is in the singular (as it regularly is in the Old Testament when it refers to a plurality of descendants). With this we may compare the argument in Heb 4:3–5 that the words of Ps 95:11 (or more precisely LXX 96:11, as we shall see): 'They shall never enter my rest' means an entry into God's own post-creation rest. This depends on the fact that the word 'my' (which in Hebrew is of course merely the enclitic *yod*) can mean either 'the rest that I give' or 'the rest I enjoy'. The argument further rests upon a translation detail: the LXX uses the verb *katapauō* in Gn 2:2 and the noun *katapausis* in the psalm; the *Textus Massoreticus* uses two words: *shabath* and, in the psalm, *menuhah*.[31]

With this we may compare another argument much more central to Hebrews, which rests upon a (negative) descriptive detail; the well-known argument of 7:3, which is widely acknowledged to be 'allegorical' (eg by Spicq and Héring *comm in loc*). Since Gn 14 does not provide any ancestry for Melchizedek, and the lack is not filled up by any later text, Hebrews produces an argument remarkably similar to the rabbinic 'what does not find mention in Torah may be taken not to exist' (*quod non in Tora non in mundo*): 'He is without father or mother or genealogy, and has neither beginning of days nor end of life . . . (7:3).

This argument upon a descriptive detail, after a fashion which appears to be quite arbitrary in terms of modern, scientific, exegetical procedures, is of great structural importance in Hebrews. It is taken

[31] Bruce, *comm in loc*, quite correctly.

up in 7:15-17: 'This becomes even more evident
when another priest arises in the likeness of Melchizedek, who has become a priest, not according to
a legal requirement concerning bodily descent but
by the power of an indestructible life. For it is witnessed of him: Thou art a priest for ever, after the
order of Melchizedek.' It underlies 7:23-25 in
which the phrase 'for ever' is repeated: 'The former
priests were many in number, because they were
prevented by death from continuing in office; but
he holds his priesthood permanently, because he
continues for ever. Consequently he is able for all
time to save those who draw near to God through
him, since he always lives to make intercession for
them.' The order of Melchizedek is, for Hebrews,
an eternal order; this is established by his rabbinical
exegesis of Gn 14. And if one follows the shift from
eis ton aiōna ('for ever') to the adjective *aiōnios*
('eternal'), the theme of the eternal, Melchizedek
character of Christ's priesthood is built into the
structure of 9:11-14, which Vanhoye's literary analysis has shown to be the centre of the central section of the entire epistle. Heb 9:13-14 runs: 'For if
the sprinkling of defiled persons with the blood of
goats and bulls and with the ashes of a heifer sanctifies for the purification of the flesh, how much more
shall the blood of Christ, who through the eternal
Spirit offered himself without blemish to God, purify

your conscience from dead works to serve the living God.'[32]

(f) When Barr speaks of situation similarities in style and language he is thinking of implicit references by New Testament writers to the Old in the way in which they describe New Testament situations. I have not found precisely that usage in Hebrews: there is, however, a variant type in which an Old Testament situation is re-described in such a way (at least according to many exegetes)[33] that it refers implicitly to a New Testament situation. I am thinking of 9:20 in which Moses' covenant saying is changed from 'Behold the blood of the covenant which the Lord has made with you in accordance with all these words' (Ex 24:8) to 'This is the blood of the covenant which God commanded you', where the change from 'Behold' to 'This' seems to echo Jesus' saying over the cup at the last supper.

(g) The apparent sounding beforehand, in a description derived from Ex 24:8, of the words of Jesus over the cup is made possible here because Jesus' words are a deliberate echo of Moses' words. There is thus a situation similarity in action latent in the text of Heb 9:20. It is possible, further, that Hebrews understands Jesus' willing suffering out-

---

[32] Spicq, *comm in loc*, supports his interpretation of 'the eternal spirit' with references to 7:16 and 24. The parallelism remains whether one thinks of 'spirit' or 'Spirit'.

[33] So, eg Spicq, Héring, *comm in loc*, and as a possibility Bruce, 208, n 109.

side the gate of Jerusalem as a willed fulfilment of
the rubric in Leviticus for the day of atonement:
'the bodies of those animals whose blood is brought
into the sanctuary by the high priest as a sacrifice
for sin are burned outside the camp' (Heb 13 : 11).[34]

(h) I have already indicated that I regard the application of Jer 31 : 31ff to the new covenant mediated by Christ as an example of the transference of
prophecy (Heb 8 : 6–13). The two proof texts in
5 : 5–6 should also be considered here, since they are
generally recognised as oracles occurring within
psalms, possibly spoken by court prophets. Ps 2 has
been very variously dated; E. Podechard[35] thinks of a
first creation in honour of one of the kings between
Solomon and the exile, and a second edition with
the addition of the phrase 'against the Lord and his
anointed' after the exile but before the LXX translation. The original psalm, he thinks, was created for
the day of the enthronement of the king, and verse
7 expresses the divine adoptive sonship of the kings
of Judah, after the promise of 2 Sa 7 : 14. Though
Ps 2 : 7 is oracular, it is hardly a fore-telling, since
the adoption coincides with the enthronement. Even
if one regards the re-edition as changing the whole
meaning of the psalm, as Podechard seems to, there
can be no doubt that the psalm is still understood
in a thoroughly political sense: there is thus trans-

---

[34] Spicq, *in loc.*
[35] *Le Psautier*, 2 vols (Lyons 1949 and 1954), *comm in loc.*

ference in time and transference in the very meaning of kingship. I suggest that Jesus' kingship is not of this world (Jn 18 : 36) because it is an 'allegorical'-typological kingship.

The famous Ps 110, the first verse of which is already quoted in the gospels (Mk 12 : 36, par), is placed by Podechard in the time of David, not as part of an enthronement ceremony, as other scholars think, but in connection with the taking of Jerusalem, the bringing in of the ark and the assumption by David of the priestly prerogatives of the old Jebusaean priest-kings.[36] The oracle of 110 : 4 is therefore not the foretelling of some future event but the justification of a *fait accompli*; though naturally the consequences for the future are enormous. It is clear, in any case, that an element of transference is involved in its use in Hebrews: and this is *the* proof-text of Hebrews.

(i) There can be no doubt that non-prophetic texts are given value as prophecies in Hebrews. The use of Ps 8 in chapter 2 is a certain case of this. The citation of Ps 40 : 6–8 in chapter 10 is surely another. Ps 40 is not, in its original literary setting, a prophecy, nor does it contain oracles. But there is a still more extraordinary procedure in the citation and application of Ps 40 that is better examined under our next heading.

[36] *Comm in loc.*

(j) The changing or cutting short of texts is a constant element in Hebrews.[37] The most important example of this, structurally,[38] occurs at 10:5-10 where a passage from a psalmist who shows a total detachment from the sacrificial cult and a marked preference for the observance of the (moral, surely?) law is interpreted in a 'cultic' sense. Vanhoye sees this passage as an exposition of the effects of the sacrifice of Christ, on the basis of the announcement of the three-fold theme of the great central (third) part of the epistle in 5:9-10: 'high priest after the order of Melchizedek'—chapter 7; 'being made perfect'—chapters 8 and 9; 'salvation'—10:1-18. It is true that the formal link is provided by the single word 'salvation', in the first announcement of the theme in 5:9 and in the repeated announcement of the theme in 9:28; but its meaning in those two verses may give us some hint of its meaning in 10:1-18.

In 5:9 the full phrase is 'source of eternal salvation'; the word 'source' points to Jesus himself, it is only the following phrase 'to all who obey him' that points to those who are the objects of Jesus' work of salvation. And in the small-scale parallelisms that Vanhoye rightly discerns in 5:7-10 'source of eternal *salvation*' is an echo of 'to him who was able to *save* him from death'.[39] There is therefore an em-

[37] J. Thomas, 'The Old Testament citations in Hebrews', *New Testament Studies* II (1965), 303-325.

[38] Vanhoye, 165. 55.

[39] *Ib*, 109-110.

phasis laid upon the death of Christ. Heb 9:28 runs:
'so Christ having been offered once to bear the sins
of many, will appear a second time, not to deal with
sin but to *save* those who are eagerly waiting for
him.' 'Christ, having been offered once' is echoed in
10:10 'through the offering of the body of Jesus
Christ once for all', while 'those who are eagerly
waiting for him' are the 'we' of 10:10: 'by that will
we have been sanctified'. It is no wonder that Vanhoye, who has revealed to us so many parallelisms in
Hebrews, should appear to have missed these. They
are important for the meaning of 10:1–10 in relation to the epistle as a whole. It is, in fact, impossible
to think of the saving efficacy of the death of Christ
apart from his willing endurance of that death in
obedience to the Father's will. 'And by that will'
both 'we have been sanctified'—the effect of Christ's
sacrifice—and 'through the offering of the body of
Jesus Christ once for all'—it was God's will that
Jesus should endure the bodily agony of the cross.

Vanhoye has put this very clearly in his detailed
analysis of 10:1–10: Hebrews 'notes precisely that
this *will* is a new arrangement which replaces the
law' and 10:10b 'shows us, finally, what the decisive
intervention is that suppresses the old cult and takes
its place: *the offering of the body of Jesus Christ
once for all*'.[40] I emphasise the relationship of 10:1–
10 to the general structure because the importance

[40] *Op cit*, 165.

of Ps 40 : 6–8 is that it is a proof-text with a structural role to play in Hebrews as a whole.

Further, in Heb 3 : 7–4, 11 the disobedience of the fathers in the desert is held up as a warning example to Christians. In contrast it is said of Christ in 5 : 8, immediately preceding the announcement of the themes of 7–10, 18, that 'Although he was a Son, he learned obedience through what he suffered'. There is no direct, formal, linguistic link between obedience (*hupakoē*) and will (*thelēma*) but the conceptual one can hardly be doubted. I see this as touching on 10 : 1–10 formally speaking, through the word 'salvation': Jesus is, in the providence and will of God, a source of salvation through his obedience unto death.

Ps 40 : 6–8, then, as it is cited in 10 : 5–7, is a proof-text with a structural importance for Hebrews. It is disconcerting to find that it can be made to work in this way at all only through the suppression of Ps 40 : 8b: 'thy law is within my heart'. For Hebrews, 'when there is a change in the priesthood, there is necessarily a change in the law as well'. Hebrews cannot therefore cite verse 8b of the psalm. 'What is one to make of the subjection of the text to such treatment? At first sight one is inclined to be indignant . . .', Vanhoye suggests[41]; it certainly does call for some explanation. Vanhoye himself continues:

[41] *Op cit*, 166.

'but undoubtedly it is better to take a second look before launching into a harsh criticism'. His own exegesis is in line with that offered by Bonsirven and Spicq, not only in relation to this passage but in relation to Hebrews as a whole: the sacrifice of Christ, which is taken quite literally as a bloody sacrifice, the slaughter of a sacrificial victim, infinitely transcends the Old Testament sacrifices since Jesus was both priest and victim, 'he entered once for all into the Holy Place, taking (RSV footnote: Greek 'through') not the blood of goats and calves but his own blood' (9. 12).

The difficulty with this exegesis, which enables one to claim that Hebrews is in line with the fundamental intention of the psalmist, ie to reject merely external sacrifice, is that in attempting to meet the interpretative criticism of the psalmist (for, in fact, he does not tell us why God does not desire sacrifice and offering) it seems to fall inevitably back into a pre-pentateuchal and pagan conception of what kind of sacrifice is pleasing to God. It is difficult to accept that Hebrews, in evoking the sacrifice of Isaac in 11 : 17–19, as a pre-figuring of the sacrifice and resurrection of Christ,[42] does not recall the original point of the story (however much Gn 22 : 1–19 is now a story of the dialectic of faith, promise, obedience and the son of blessing[43]) that God takes no

[42] Vanhoye, Bruce, Héring, *comm in loc.*
[43] Von Rad, *Genesis*, Eng tr, London 1961, *in loc.*

delight in human sacrifice, however voluntary (cf Ex
13:11–16, 2 Kg 21:6 (Manasses!) etc).

It would seem preferable, therefore, to suppose
that though Hebrews finds in Ps 40:6–8a a proof-
text with complete probative force for himself and
his readers, nevertheless he is aware of the distance
between his meaning, in which the law is primarily
the ritual, sacrificial, priestly law, and the meaning
of the psalmist, who opposes law and sacrifice.
Hebrews is fully aware that his exploitation of
the Melchizedek texts is a piece of special pleading,
to bring Melchizedek into conformity (*aphōmoiōmenos:* 'made like unto' according to Bruce: so,
equivalently, Spicq, Héring[44]) with the pre-figured
Christ. He is likewise aware of the typological
nature of his use of the high priesthood, the tent,
and its ritual: 'thus it was necessary for the copies
(*hupodeigmata*) of the heavenly things to be purified
with these rites, but the heavenly things themselves with better sacrifices than these', 9:23, and
'since the law has but a shadow (*skia*) of the good
things to come instead of the true form of these
realities, it can never, by the same sacrifices which
are continually offered year after year, make perfect
those who draw near' (10:1). I suggest that in 10:5–
10 he is able to cut short the psalm, in an admittedly
arbitrary way, because he thinks of the offering of
Christ as *typologically* an offering. We can represent

[44] Héring remarks: 'Here clearly typology slides into allegory'.

this by inverted commas: 'by that will we have been sanctified through the 'offering' of the body of Jesus Christ once for all' (10:10).

(k) Our last example of 'allegorical' procedures, the tailoring of implicit quotations to fit in with later ideas, can be dealt with more briefly and simply. Chapter 9 first evokes the liturgy of the day of atonement (9:7), then applies it to Christ (9:11–14). Verses 19–21 evoke the Sinai covenant sacrifice, though it substitutes the sprinkling of the book with blood, in place of the altar, and also the dedication of the tent with blood, though the text in Ex 40 makes no mention of a sprinkling of the tent (though Josephus does[45]). Upon all of this Hebrews remarks: 'Indeed, under the law almost everything is purified with blood, and without the shedding of blood there is no forgiveness of sins.' In this way the covenant sacrifice and the dedication ceremonies are turned, quite unhistorically, into atonement rituals.

In this list of procedures of interpretation of the New Testament upon the Old, pure typology and pure prophecy, where these can be found, stand somewhat apart from the others. The rest I shall call 'allegory' in a wider sense. The existence of 'allegorical' typology in all the crucial places in Hebrews has now been demonstrated, in a preliminary way. Something too of the cohesive structure, the seamless

[45] So eg Héring, *comm in loc.*

robe, of Hebrews as an imaginative, literary work
has been shown. The literary structure and the typology of Hebrews, particularly with regard to the
priesthood of Christ, will be more closely examined
in the next chapter. The fourth chapter will be given
to an analysis of the (realised) eschatology of
Hebrews. Let me say briefly why typology and
eschatology should be thought of in relation to one
another.[46]

The precise relationship between typology and
eschatology will naturally depend upon how one understands these two. We have seen above some of
the difficulties involved in trying to define typology,
and especially in trying to draw a firm distinction
from allegory. Eschatology has been at the centre of
the debates over the meaning of the New Testament
at least since Schweitzer demonstrated that Jesus of
Nazareth was not the gentle moralist of liberal theology but an extremely disconcerting eschatological
preacher firmly placed within first-century judaism.
From New Testament interpretation a recognition
of the importance of eschatological themes as part
of the essential structure has passed over into Old
Testament interpretation also. This is particularly
evident in the work of Von Rad. Because eschatology

---

[46] Cf G. Von Rad, 'Typological interpretation of the Old
Testament', in *Essays on Old Testament Interpretation*, ed C.
Westermann, Eng tr, London 1963, and W. Eichrodt's essay
there. Also Von Rad's *Old Testament Theology* II, Part 3,
Edinburgh-London 1965.

is so important a theme it is natural that conceptions of it should differ in detail.

Von Rad thinks of the conjunction between typology and eschatology, within the Old Testament, in terms of a pattern of likeness between the beginning-time and the end-time:

> The Old Testament, on the contrary, is dominated by an essentially different form of typological thinking, namely, that of the eschatological correspondence between beginning and end (*Urzeit und Endzeit*). Isaiah and Amos speak of the eschatological return of paradise (Is 11 : 6–8; Am 9 : 13), Amos of the return of the pristine David ('as in the days of old', Am 9 : 11, RSV), Hosea and Deutero-Isaiah of the return of the wilderness days (Hos 2 : 16–20; Is 52 : 11f), and Isaiah of the return of the old Davidic Jerusalem (Is 1 : 21–26).[47]

Von Rad remarks that the first stage of the salvation history comes to be regarded as an *Urzeit*: the passover, the desert time, David. He rejects Bultmann's criticism that this typology is nothing more than the ancient oriental theory of the cyclic occurrence of world-periods, and insists on 'the linear way from type to antitype'.[48]

By way of complement to Von Rad's presentation I should like to put forward a related but slightly

[47] Von Rad's essay in the Westermann volume, 19.
[48] *Ib*, 20.

different conception of the way in which eschatology shows itself: as the ending of one world-age and the beginning of another. This will have the advantage of justifying Von Rad's transference of *Urzeit* to the beginning of Israel's history, and of bringing the theme of judgment into better focus—Von Rad does just acknowledge its existence.[49] Perhaps the clearest example is the oracle of judgment upon Babylon in Is 13, which is normally taken as a sixth-century prophecy, dating from a time after the Medes had begun to demonstrate their power and when the neo-Babylonian empire was already falling apart. The capture of Babylon under Cyrus was in fact a very peaceful one. Is 13 presents it as a return to the primitive chaos:

> Behold, the day of the Lord comes, cruel, with wrath and fierce anger, to make the earth a desolation and to destroy its sinners from it. For the stars of the heavens and their constellations will not give their light; the sun will be dark at its rising and the moon will not shed its light. I will punish the world for its evil, and the wicked for their iniquity; I will put an end to the pride of the arrogant, and lay low the haughtiness of the ruthless. I will make men more rare than fine gold, and mankind than the gold of Ophir. Therefore I will make the heavens tremble, and the earth will be

[49] *Ib*, 36, 'In acts of judgment and acts of redemption alike, the prefiguration of the Christ-event of the New Testament'.

shaken out of its place, at the wrath of the Lord of hosts in the day of his fierce anger (Is. 13 : 9–13).

To do full justice to Von Rad's conception of *Urzeit*, one might note that the story of the absolute *Urzeit* in Gn 1 is, between the lines, the ending of one age and the beginning of another. The status of Gn 1 as a de-mythologisation of the Babylonian myth of the creation, *Enuma Elish*, is very widely acknowledged. In *Enuma Elish* the creation of the human cosmos is indeed the end of the world for Tiamat, the dark, chaotic all-mother, and her satellites.

This passage from Isaiah is echoed at Hag 2 : 6, a passage quoted in Heb 12 : 26: 'Yet once more I will shake not only the earth but also the heaven.' In Haggai the prophecy refers to the rebuilding of the temple after the return from Babylon, with the gold forthcoming after an eschatological shaking of the world and the nations. In Hebrews it is used to establish a typological parallel between the shaking of the earth at Sinai and the shaking on the day of judgment.

The theme of unrealised eschatology, that of the absolutely last day, is an important one in Hebrews.[50] But Hebrews is especially and rightly known for its stress upon realised eschatology, upon the once for

[50] See C. K. Barrett, 'The eschatology of the Epistle to the Hebrews', in *The background of the New Testament and its eschatology*, ed W. D. Davies and D. Daube, Cambridge 1956.

all appearance of Christ at the end of the age (9 : 26). It will be the task of our third chapter to show that the intertwining of typology and eschatology is found in Hebrews also, and in such a way that neither can be understood without the other.

Before closing this chapter there are, perhaps, two objections to be considered, neither of them properly exegetical. The first is that no theological statement, no fully rational communication, is possible through the language of metaphor. The second, that the literal priesthood of Christ is part of the faith and the defined doctrine of the catholic church.

The first objection has a long philosophical history behind it. Plato's exclusion of the poets from the ideal state in the *Republic*[51] is well known. Even if it is difficult to decide if Plato is entirely serious, he remarks there that the quarrel was already a long-standing one, and provides some edged quotations to prove it. Another point he makes there is the scandalous behaviour of the gods in Homer. Thus early the concern of the philosopher and moralist over the scandalous aspects of Greek myth and poetry is clearly expressed. This was a continuing preoccupation, for Homer stood at the centre of hellenistic education to the end. To meet the difficulty the philosophers and educationists developed a technique of allegorical interpretation that enabled them to deny the vices of the gods and to draw moral

[51] Book 10, 605–608.

lessons from their reported behaviour.[52] Aristotle, in his *Poetics* and elsewhere, is able to give a more positive account of poetry, and especially of drama: but he does not conceive the idea that any important statement about god or man might better be made through the medium of poetry and metaphor.

This reserve towards poetry in the Greek philosophical tradition is probably the reason why Thomas Aquinas, in his article under the title 'Should holy scripture use metaphors', after starting his *determinatio* with the observation that since it is connatural to man to proceed from objects of sense to objects of intellect it is right for scripture to make use of metaphor, can nevertheless, in his reply to the second objection, risk the statement that whatever is stated metaphorically in one place of scripture is stated literally (*expressius*) elsewhere.[53]

Perhaps this attitude, as it is found among recent thomists (and both Bonsirven and Spicq, who have written very influential commentaries upon Hebrews are in some sense thomists), has found 'classical' expression in this passage from Penido:

> The poet and the theologian are very close to one another, depending as they do upon metaphor because both of them are concerned with the extra-rational. So close and yet so distant! For

[52] See eg J. Pepin, *Mythe et allégorie*, Paris 1958; R. P. C. Hanson, *op cit*.
[53] *Summa Theologiae* 1a. 1. 9.

the poet's domain is the infra-rational, whatever cannot raise itself to the clear light of intelligence: sense objects, individuals, emotions, the movement and flow of the inner life, the palpable rhythm of time. What the poet gives us, in impressive language, is only intuitions and images of particular realities.

The theologian, on the other hand has the supra-rational as his share, that which is too full of truth to be expressed in our limited concepts. Established at the summit of immaterial reality, sweating to speak the unspeakable, the theologian has to fall back upon metaphors in order to suggest through their converging lines some of the results of his contemplation.[54]

The acceptance of metaphor is clearly less than wholehearted here, and this reserve flows out from a whole philosophy that makes hard and fast distinctions between infra-rational and supra-rational, between image and concept, between imagination and intellect, that read like naive pieces of mediaevalising. The book was written as early as 1931, but already the history of religions school had demonstrated the historical dependence of philosophy and religion upon myth, Freud and Jung had shown the myth-making structure of the unconscious mind (which is not to be identified with the *phantasia* or

[54] M. T.-L. Penido, *Le rôle de l'analogie en théologie dogmatique*, Paris 1931.

imaginatio of Aquinas,[55]) the history-centred philosophies of the nineteenth century were still under development and showing a continuing power of
illumination, personalist philosophies were flourish-
ing, and Kierkegaard, the father of existentialism,
was long dead, though not yet as popular as he was
later to become. Yet Penido's ideas still seem to
haunt thomists.

In any case, it is clear that a set of presuppositions
like those would seriously embarrass any thomist
biblical scholar (it is surely possible to study
Aquinas, even to find him one of the most fruitful
of theologians and philosophers, without clinging to
the rigid schema set out above): he is cripplingly unable to take the poetical passages of scripture as anything but a second best for the theologian and
educated man. This idea can claim the authority of
Aquinas: 'It is fitting that holy scripture, which is
addressed to all in common (according to the words
of Rm 1 : 14: I am under obligation both to the wise
and the unwise), should set forth spiritual realities
through bodily images; so that the uneducated, who
are incapable of grasping intelligible realities in
themselves (*secundum se*), should be able to grasp
them in this way at least.'[56]

What would become of the Old Testament sagas
and histories, the psalms and the prophecies, of the

---

[55] *Summa Theologiae* 1a. 78. 4.
[56] 1a. 1. 9. c.

gospel parables, the sermon on the mount, and the eschatological discourse, if we were to take them seriously as a second best? And what of Hebrews, with its tightly woven literary structure, a work of art like a church or a piece of music (whether one judges it to be a success, in accordance with one's own taste, or not), with its elaborate, and sometimes extravagant use of typology and 'allegory'? The best response to this objection is perhaps, finally, to meet affirmation with affirmation: 'myth' and 'poetry' (I use these terms in a wide sense), on the one hand, and philosophy and theology, on the other, are not exclusive systems but rather friendly rivals, who will constantly need to borrow one another's clothes. Some aspects of our apprehensions of the mystery of God and of the meaning of human existence are best set out in abstract philosophical and theological language, while some of man's deepest perceptions have been reached and expressed poetically. Let us keep an open mind as to whether Hebrews may not be just such a poetic imaging forth of the mystery of Christ.[57]

[57] Protestant scholars are, in general, more ready than catholics to acknowledge that metaphor runs right through Hebrews. However M. Richard, in his *Le mystère de la redemption*, Tournai-Paris 1959, has a brief section on Hebrews in which he speaks in an apparently unrestricted way of the 'allegorical method' of the author (p 68) and of allegorical exegesis opening up in a way into the christian mystery (p 70). Spicq himself, in the first volume of his commentary, offers a de-typologisation of Hebrews: 'These, obviously, are only metaphors in need of great

The second objection runs that the literal priest-hood of Christ is part of the faith and defined doc-trine of the catholic church. So, for example, Spicq, in a review of a book by Ph.-H. Menoud, can quote the author as saying 'Only Jesus is priest in the full and proper sense of the word' and comment upon this 'that is what the catholic faith confesses'.[58] I would agree with both Menoud and Spicq here if we could take 'full' in the New Testament sense of 'fulfilment' and note that Hebrews never speaks of a fulfilment of the levitical priesthood, though one could make out a case for regarding the priesthood of Christ as a 'fulfilment' of the Melchizedek order of priesthood; and if one were to give 'proper' the New Testament meaning of 'true' (alēthinos), as in Heb 8:2: 'a minister in the sanctuary and the true tent which is set up not by man but by the Lord' called in 9:11 'the greater and more perfect tent (not made with hands, that is, not of this creation)' which is the risen body of Christ,[59] and as in Jn 15:1: 'I am the true vine, and my Father is the vine-

---

purification. (4) Thus: blood equals life; the high priest, the in-carnate Son of God; the order of Melchizedek, the eternal priest-hood; sacrifice, offering; altar, cross; holy of holies, the presence of God in heaven...' (I, 314). Since 'offering' is not, apparently, a sacrifice, only the eternal priesthood remains untouched, surely for extra-exegetical reasons.

[58] Spicq, review of Menoud's *L'Eglise et les ministères selon le N.T.*, in *Revue des Sciences Philosophiques et Théologiques* XXXIV (1950), 36.

[59] Vanhoye, 157, n 1.

dresser'. 'Fulfilment' and 'truth' are not, in the New Testament, words serving for a logical and philosophico-theological affirmation of literalness, as contrasted with metaphor: they point rather to the transcendence of the mystery of Christ.

There is always a danger, in theological exegesis, of searching among the biblical images and symbols for a literal proposition that one can get one's teeth into. As J. Moffat remarked more than forty years ago:

> While the author of *Pros Hebraious* often turned the literal into the figurative, his theological interpreters have been as often engaged in turning the figurative expressions of the epistle into what was literal. A due appreciation of the symbolism has been the slow gain of the historical method as applied to the classics of primitive christianity. There is no consistent symbolism, indeed, not even in the case of the *archiereus*; in the nature of the case, there could not be. But symbolism there is, and symbolism of a unique kind.

And a little later he speaks of Hebrews'

> genuinely primitive faith in Jesus as the one mediator. The ideas of the perfect Priest and the perfect Sacrifice are a theological expression, in symbolic language, of what was vital to the classical piety of the early church; and apart from Paul

no one set this out so cogently or clearly as the writer of *Pros Hebraious*.[60]

There is room for deepening Moffat's 'due appreciation' still further, for giving a more profound philosophical account of the role of symbol and image in all human thinking,[61] but his remarks are sound enough as far as they go.

The idea that the literal priesthood of Christ is a defined doctrine of the catholic church is usually supported (by, for example, Spicq and Bonsirven) by a reference to two texts, one from the council of Ephesus, the other from Trent. I should like to preface my examination of these texts with an eminently sensible observation by P. Fannon in an issue of the *Clergy Review*:

> While one must safeguard the Church's dogmas, it is legitimate to try to investigate their formulation and the commentaries given on them by theologians. That formulation may owe much to the historical circumstances (eg of polemic) in which it arose and thus the formulation must be intepreted according to those circumstances. The *ad hoc* discussions preceding such a formulation are immensely important for delineating the sense and limits of that formula. And even when the

[60] J. Moffatt, *The Epistle to the Hebrews*, Edinburgh 1924. introd, 31, 39.
[61] See eg the last part of J. Pepin's *Mythe et Allégorie*.

3+

history behind the formula is ascertained, the text must be examined, distinguishing what is introductory, what is doctrine, what is digression and what is the authentic meaning at stake.[62]

Fannon, in the same part of his article, remarks that this is to extend to the dogmas of the church the methods of interpretation accepted for exegesis of scripture. These methods have been recommended to us, for responsible use, naturally, in the Biblical Commission's *Instruction on the gospels* of 1964 and in Vatican II's *Constitution on Divine Revelation*. Unless we are willing to extend these same methods of interpretation to the definitions of councils, I do not see how we can make the same *Constitution*'s statement that the *Magisterium* (teaching authority of the church) is not above the word of God but serves it (chapter 2) a reality for us.

If, with these observations in mind, we approach the two conciliar texts that speak of the priesthood of Christ, we find that neither of them is addressed to the question as to whether the priesthood of Christ is a literal one or one of the great biblical images expressive of his mystery.

The passage in Ephesus[63] referred to is the tenth

[62] P. Fannon, 'The Dutch Catechism: its hidden persuaders', in *Clergy Review* (January 1968), 3–13.

[63] I leave aside the difficult historical question whether the letter and the anathemas of Cyril are properly part of the acts of Ephesus or not, and whether, if they were, their reception makes

anathema of Cyril against Nestorius. After references to Heb 3 : 1 and Eph 5 : 2 it goes on:

> If therefore anyone says that it was not the Word
> of God himself who was made our high priest and
> apostle, when he 'was made flesh' and a man like
> us, but another distinct man besides him (born)
> from woman, or if anyone says that he offered
> himself as an offering for himself, and not rather
> for us alone (for not knowing sin he needed no
> offering), let him be anathema.

It is clear that this text is directed to the disputation
with Nestorius, affirming that Jesus was not a man
and person alongside the word of God, who needed,
because he was a creature who fell short of the holi-
ness of God, to offer sacrifice for himself. The nature
of the priesthood of Christ and of his sacrifice are
not at issue; indeed literalist interpreters would do
well to look again at the placing of Eph 5 : 2 alongside Heb 3 : 1: Christ 'gave himself up for us, a frag-
rant offering and sacrifice to God'—this is clearly
an image drawn from the Jewish ritual of sacrifice.

If we turn to the passage from the council of

---

the anathemas of Cyril anathemas of the council. The definition
of faith of Chalcedon seems merely to make reference to the letter
of Cyril; only with Constantinople 2 do we find the round statement that it, with the anathemas, is part of the acts of Ephesus.
See *Conciliorum Oecumenicorum Decreta*, edited by the *Istituto
per le Scienze Religiose* of Bologna, Friburg-Rome 962, 33.

Trent to which we are referred, session 22, chapter 1, and canons 1 and 4, we find that here and throughout the work of the session the subject was that of the sacrifice of the mass, not directly that of the sacrifice of Christ or of his priesthood. The canons, which alone bind the faith of members of the church under pain of anathema, run as follows. Canon 1: 'If anyone shall say that in the Mass a true and proper sacrifice is not offered to God, or that to offer is only to give us Christ to be eaten, let him be anathema.' And the 4th canon: 'If anyone shall say that the sacrifice of the Mass constitutes a blasphemy against the holy sacrifice of the cross offered by Christ, or that it derogates from it, let him be anathema.' It is clear from these passages that the point at issue is the identity of the sacrifice of the mass with the sacrifice of Calvary, a sacramental identity, naturally, since the mass is not a mere memorial of Calvary but an effective sign of the sacrifice of Calvary. The authoritative explanation of the canons in the doctrinal chapters is still directed throughout to the reformation polemic against the mass. The first chapter is largely based upon Hebrews, but it does not seem that it was the intention of the fathers to define any particular exegesis of Hebrews. In the light of this and the other chapters it is surely legitimate to take the 'true and proper sacrifice' of the first dogmatic canon as an affirmation of the sacramental identity of the sacrifice of the mass with that of the cross.[64] It would take very careful historical proofs to show that the fathers intended to demand, for the true sacrifice of the cross upon which the true sacrifice of the mass depends absolutely, any further 'truth' than that claimed by the New Testament.

It may appear to some readers that this approach to the statements of Trent is an unduly minimising one. The idea that one cannot bind the faith of members of the church in uncertain matters is, in fact, by no means foreign to the mind of the fathers of

[64] That responsible catholic theologians have ever spoken of the mass as a repetition of the sacrifice of the cross is often taken to be a protestant *canard*, but let us be fair and consider eg the article of M. Fraeyman, 'La spiritualisation de l'idée du Temple dans les épîtres pauliniennes', in *Ephemerides Theologicae Lovanienses* XXIII (1947), 378–412: 'Undoubtedly, the Jewish Temple and material cult have become fundamentally useless through the power of the death and resurrection of Christ, which has established a New Covenant. However, this does not in the least exclude the possibility that Christ laid down the principles of a new, external, Christian cult. The death of Christ is not merely conceived of as a sacrifice, it is a true sacrifice that the faithful must repeat (*répéter*) in memory of Christ (Lk 21:19). That is what the Pauline churches did in their celebration of the Supper (Ac 9:13; 1 Cor 10:14-22, 11:26-32). If here the idea of sacrifice is spiritualised in being applied to the death of Christ, an external cultic and ritual expression is not therefore excluded, on the contrary, this sacrifice must be fulfilled (*doit s'accomplir*) externally.' Fraeyman is arguing against Wenschkewitz, 'Die Spiritualisierung der Kultusbegriffe Tempel, Priester und Opfer im Neuen Testament', in *Angelos* IV, 4 (1932), 71–230. I see no difficulty in acknowledging a dominically founded eucharistic cult that is an effective anamnesis of the typological 'sacrifice' of the cross.

Trent. The initial drafts of the statement on the
mass had appeared to support a theory that the last
supper constituted a sacrifice distinct from that of
the cross: immediately Peter Soto,[65] and Jerome Seri-
pandus, papal legate at the council (and therefore
in a document for the declaration of his conscience,
since he would not be able to intervene in the debates in support of this),[66] came out strongly against
a teaching that was not sufficiently founded in scripture, in the fathers, nor in the theologians. In *dubiis
libertas* is indeed part of our catholic tradition.

It is of course possible, logically and historically,
that the fathers of Trent presupposed that Christ's
sacrifice was a literal sacrifice, and further that his
priesthood was a literal priesthood. These are two
presuppositions, not one, in biblical as in other
terms, since sacrifice is not necessarily the preroga-
tive, nor even the main function, of priests. Abraham was not, save in late Jewish tradition,[67] a priest
and yet Genesis is full of stories of the sacrifices he
offered. And the original liturgy for passover, before
the book of Deuteronomy came in with its law of the

---

[65] *Concilium Tridentinum, Diariorum, Actorum, Epistularum
Tractatuum*, ed Societas Goerresiana, XIII, 1, Friburg 1938, 730–
731.

[66] *Ib*, 732–735.

[67] In the *Midrashim* Melchizedek is said to have lost his eternal
priesthood to Abraham for having named Abraham before God
(Gn 14:19). This idea seems to spring out of disputations with
christian melchizedekians, whether the church or the sect, and
possibly with a jewish gnostic sect. See eg Héring, *op cit*, 66.

single sanctuary, clearly lays down that each house-holder is to sacrifice the lamb for his family. If, however, it could be shown that the fathers of Trent held these two presuppositions, it would still need to be proved that they are true and part of catholic faith. In the apparent absence of any determination of the matter by the teaching authority of the church, the question remains open. Any attempt to give an answer will, obviously, rest largely upon Hebrews. Let us now turn to an examination of the typological element in the priesthood of Christ according to Hebrews.

3
The priesthood of Christ in Hebrews: literary structure and 'allegorical' typology

Introduction: 1:1-4

The finely shaped paragraph, 1:1-4, which introduces Hebrews, while naturally having a particularly close connection with the first part,[1] 1:5-2, 18, provides a summary presentation of the themes of the entire epistle.[2] The name which the Son has obtained is the mystery of his person and his work, he is at once Son (1:5), God (1:8-9), Lord (1:10, 2:3), the one who sits at God's right hand (1:13) and also high priest (2:17).[3] The work of the high priest is

[1] For all questions of structure I follow the brilliant demonstration and proof of this given by A. Vanhoye in his *La structure littéraire de l'Epître aux Hébreux*. Other scholars had worked on this before him, most successfully L. Vaganay, 'Le plan de l'Epître aux Hébreux', in *Mémorial Lagrange*, Paris 1940, 269-277, but Vanhoye's much longer work supersedes all others.

[2] Vanhoye, 241-243. See also his article 'De christologia a qua initium sumit Epistula ad Hebraeos', in *Verbum Domini* XLIII (1965), 3-14, 49-61, 113-123.

[3] Vanhoye, 38.

already spoken of in the phrase 'When he had made purification (*katharismos*) for sins' (1 : 3). In 9 : 13 we read that 'the sprinkling of defiled persons with the blood of goats and bulls and with the ashes of a heifer sanctifies for the purification (*katharotēs*) of the flesh' and in the next verse 'how much more shall the blood of Christ, who through the eternal Spirit offered himself without blemish to God, purify (*katharizō*) your conscience from dead works to serve the living God'. The paragraph 9 : 11–14 is revealed by Vanhoye's analysis as the literary and thematic centre of the whole epistle.[4] Nor does the idea of purification end there: 'Indeed, under the law almost everything is purified (*katharizō*) with blood, and without the shedding of blood there is no forgiveness of sins. Thus it was necessary for the copies of the heavenly things to be purified (*katharizō*) with these rites, but the heavenly things themselves with better sacrifices than these' (9 : 21–22). 10 : 2 reminds us of the inability of the sacrifices of the law to purify (*katharizō*) the worshippers; and at 10 : 22 the water of baptism is called pure (*katharos*) because of its power to make hearts pure in virtue of the blood of Christ: 'With our hearts sprinkled clean from an evil conscience and our bodies washed with pure water.' The parallelism of the two phrases leaps to the eye, the inward grace of baptism

---

[4] Vanhoye, 237–239.

3*

corresponds to the outer sacrament.[5] 'Sprinkle', 'conscience' and 'pure' are a deliberate echo of 9:13–14. In this way the 'purification' of 1:3 leads into the heart of the epistle.

There is a clear parallel in 1:3 between the priesthood and the kingship of Christ. This parallelism is one of the characteristics of the epistle: in 2:9 Jesus is crowned with glory and honour,[6] after (2:10) being made perfect (*teleioō*), a priestly word, through suffering; in 5:5–6 a royal messianic text is placed alongside the Melchizedek text; in 8:1 the high priest is 'seated at the right hand of the throne of the Majesty in heaven'; and in 10:12–13 'But when Christ (RSV footnote: Greek *this one*) had offered for all time a single sacrifice for sins, he sat down at the right hand of God, then to wait until his enemies should be made a stool for his feet'. Since the kingdom of Jesus is not of this world (Jn 18:36), and the only crown he ever wore on earth was the

[5] Vanhoye, 175–177. He attaches the first phrase to the verb 'draw near' and the second to 'hold fast' for reasons of stylistic symmetry. On p 174 he sees a link between the 'sprinkling' of 10:22 and 9:19. He does not refer 10:22 to 9:13–14, as I do.

[6] Vanhoye, after Michel, notes that the phrase 'glory and honour' is applied to a man only here in Ps 8 and at Ex 28:2, 40 in the LXX, and that in Heb 5:4–5 honour (*timē*) and glory (in the verb form *doxazō*) are used of Aaron and Christ; *op cit*, 83, n 1. 'Crowned with glory and honour' is perhaps both a royal and a priestly phrase, since 'crown' and 'to crown' (*stephanos* and *stephanoō*) are used predominantly of kings in the LXX though there are some priestly exceptions: Zech 6:11, 14; Ecclus 45:12; 1 Mc 10:20.

crown of thorns (Mk 15:17), it can reasonably be urged that the kingship of Jesus, as of his Father, is one of the great biblical images. Now 'purification' is clearly a metaphor, though perhaps a dead or dying one, in its ritual and ethical use. When we note that Jesus would not be a priest at all if he were on earth (8:4), and that he purifies both consciences (9:14) and heavenly things (9:23), we may well ask if priesthood, like kingship, is not one of the great biblical symbols, and none the less irreplaceable for being so.[7]

First part: 'a name more excellent than the angels", 1:5–2:18.

Verse 4 introduces the theme of the name of Jesus which is set out in the first part of the epistle: 1:5–2:18. There is an inclusion on the word 'angels' at 1:5 (in the Greek) and 2:16. There are three main paragraphs: 1:5–14, which is concerned with the divine and kingly name of Jesus; 2:1–4, a short exhortation to attend to the gospel message; and 2:5–16, which are concerned with the themes of suffering, glory and deliverance and the priestly and redemptive verses of conclusion and transition, 17–18, are in particularly close relation.[8]

[7] Vanhoye, *art cit*, 58, says that 'the cultic themes attain their perfect fulfilment in Christ; ie they are not taken over unchanged, but are transformed in an unheard-of manner'. I suggest that this transformation is that of literal fact into biblical image.

[8] Vanhoye, *op cit*, 69–85.

It is naturally the third paragraph and the conclusion that concern us here. We have already seen
that Ps 8, which is originally a psalm about man,
closely parallel in meaning to Gn 1 : 26–30, is taken
by Hebrews as a prophecy about Jesus. Verse 8 is,
in fact, ambiguous: the words 'As it is, we do not yet
see everything in subjection to him' can refer either
to man or to Jesus.[9] Vanhoye's structural analysis
reveals two short sentences that enclose the psalm,
verse 5 and the middle part of verse 8, that provide
an inclusion on the words 'subjected' and 'subjection'. This makes it clear that 8bc is simply a preliminary comment on the psalm, preparing for the
application to Jesus,[10] while the interpretation
proper commences at 8d and runs on to 9, taking up
the various elements of the psalm: 'everything in
subjection to him' and 'for a little while was made
lower than the angels' and 'crowned with glory and
honour'. This makes it likely that all three elements
are applied directly to Jesus, for has he not 'sat down
at the right hand of God, then to wait until his

[9] See Westcott, Moffatt, NEB and Bruce for the first interpretation, Spicq and Héring for the reference to Jesus. Bruce comments that 'in any case Christ is in view as the representative
Man', and after a reference to 10:13 goes on to say 'So, while
man is primarily indicated by *autō*, the Son of Man cannot be
totally excluded from its scope.'

[10] This is part of the exegetical method of Hebrews. Compare
the way in which the Melchizedek of Gn 14 is 'made like unto'
(RSV 'resembling') (7:3), the Son of God in the preliminary
comments on the text of Genesis.

enemies should be made a stool for his feet' (10:12b–13)? We do not yet see everything subjected to Jesus for they have not yet been fully subjected. The text is therefore taken as a direct prophecy, not merely through Jesus' representative character.

We have already noted that the words 'glory and honour' have aaronic connotations in the bible. Here we must note that for Jesus this is 'because of the suffering of death, so that by the grace of God he might taste death for everyone'. The theme of suffering as the way to glory, perfection, sanctity, and liberation from death are developed in 1:10–16, together with the theme of sharing in flesh and blood, in suffering, and in death. Of special interest to us is the introduction of the theme of perfection, which is to run through the epistle: it is announced in 5:9 and 7:28 as the theme of the second section of the third part, ie 8:1–9, 28, and runs on into the later parts of the epistle, eg 10:1, 14; 11:40; 12:2, 23: Christ is himself made perfect through suffering, 2:10, and become the perfecter of those who are sanctified (10:14), which includes the just and faithful ones of the Old Testament (11:40). The word 'perfection' (*teleiōsis*) and 'to perfect' (*teleioō*) have priestly connections; where the Hebrew speaks of the 'filling of the hand' the Septuagint speaks of the 'perfecting of the hands' of priests in the ordination ritual, eg Ex 29:22, 26, 27, 29, 31, 33, 34, 35. This connection has rightly been remarked by a number of commentators.[11]

Jesus is the pioneer of our salvation (2 : 10), he who sanctifies us (2 : 11). He is able to do this because he shares a common origin with us (the commentators are divided between God, supposing that the phrase looks back to he who brings many sons to glory (2 : 10), and Adam, supposing that the phrase looks forward to 'since therefore the children share in flesh and blood, he himself likewise partook of the same nature' (2 : 14), participation in flesh and blood, and as a consequence our whole human experience, including temptation but not sin (2 : 18; 4 : 15), and even death itself (2 : 14; 9 : 11ff). The theme of Jesus' sharing in our temptations is most intimately connected with the merciful nature of our high priest (2 : 17). This verse is an announcement of the double theme of the second part of the epistle: Jesus is a faithful high priest (3 : 1–4, 14),[12] and a merciful high priest (4 : 15–5 : 10). Jesus is merciful and able to help us because he himself has suffered and been tempted (2 : 18; 4 : 15ff). The theme of the

[11] Eg Spicq, I, 282, n 6, and II, 221; Vanhoye, 43, 83. Bruce, 105, gives a double meaning to the 'made perfect' of 5 : 9: (i) he became the source of eternal salvation, (ii) he was designated high priest. This shows the connection between perfection and priesthood, but curiously neglects the announcements of the themes here; although Vanhoye's book is given in the bibliography no reference is made to it in the text.

[12] This division, following Vanhoye, will be justified at the beginning of the discussion of the second part.

high priesthood, introduced here for the first time, is not, properly speaking, the subject of the second part, but rather of the third as we shall see.

But before we leave the first part something should be said of the introduction of the theme of high priesthood. Some interpreters, eg A. J. B. Higgins,[13] have found the introduction a sudden one, and have supposed that it must therefore have been a theme already familiar to christians. When one has traced the anticipations in 'purification' (1 : 3), 'glory and honour' (2 : 9) and 'perfect' (2 : 10), the appearance of the 'high priest' at 2 : 17 seems a perfectly natural one, and it is not necessary to appeal to any previous knowledge. The theme is, in any case, sounded only in a preliminary way here, the full development is found only in the third part.

Second part: the merciful and faithful high priest, 3: 1–4: 14

Chapter 3 and the first part of chapter 4 are clearly concerned with faithfulness and obedience and their opposites unfaithfulness and disobedience; the second part of chapter 4 and the first part of chapter

---

[13] A. J. B. Higgins in an article 'The priestly Messiah', in *New Testament Studies* XIII (1963), 235: 'The suddenness with which the notion of Jesus as a "merciful and faithful high priest" is first introduced in 2 : 17 suggests that it is no invention of the writer, but was a belief already familiar to christians.' Higgins will acknowledge innovation only in the use of Ps 110:4 as a proof text of the priesthood of Christ.

5 with mercy, sympathy, temptation and suffering: these are the themes announced in 2 : 17. Vanhoye rightly divides the two sections into 3 : 1–4 : 14, with inclusion on the words 'Jesus', 'high priest' and 'confession', and 4 : 15–5 : 10, with an inclusion on 'high priest' and 'sympathise' (*sumpathēsai*) and 'suffer' (*epathen*). It is part of the literary method of Hebrews that a verse or verses ending a section or sub-section should both bring a passage to a conclusion and provide a smooth transition to the new section. This explains why commentators (eg Bruce) and translations (RSV) break after verse 13. On formal grounds Vanhoye's division seems unshakeable.

The first section of the second part does not call for very close examination here. The statement that Jesus is the apostle and high priest of our confession (3 : 1), and the exhortation 'Since then we have a great high priest who has passed through the heavens, Jesus, the Son of God, let us hold fast our confession' led Spicq to think that the high priesthood of Jesus was part of the confession of faith of the 'Hebrews'. This is a doubtful conclusion; by parallel reasoning the apostleship of Jesus should be part of the confessional formula. Now it is true that the theme of the sending of Jesus by his Father is known both in the synoptic (eg Mk 9 : 37) and Johannine (eg 12 : 44) traditions; it does not seem, however, that the word 'apostle' is used of Jesus ex-

cept in this passage.[14] Further, the apprehensiveness
about how his teaching will be received, which is
apparent in the exhortatory section with which the
third part opens, ie 5:11–6:20, suggests that more
than the particular Melchizedek, high priest and
covenant typologies are new (and we have no reason
to suppose that the 'allegorical' methods of exegesis
through which these were expounded would have
presented a particular difficulty for the readers of
Hebrews), it is rather the basic idea of priesthood
itself. One could make out a more plausible case for
supposing that the difficulty is not the conception of
Christ's priesthood, which, on this theory, would be
part of the confession of faith, but rather the necessary consequence of this: the abolition (10:9) of sacrifice, priesthood, altar and temple. But does not historical probability and the actual unfolding of the
history of the apostolic church as we can glimpse
this in Acts suggest a different development: as christians were more and more excommunicated from
Jewish community life and worship so they became,

[14] No passage listed under *apostolos* in the Moulton and Geden
concordance, apart from this one, refers to Jesus. K. H. Rengstorf,
in the article *apostolos* in TWNT, twice declares that only in
Heb 3:1 is Jesus called an apostle (I, 423 and 444). Spicq points
out that rabbinical sources (Yoma 1:5) speak of the high priest
on the day of atonement as the 'apostle of the house of Judgment' and therefore suggests a priestly interpretation of 'apostle'
in 3:1. It seems better, with Rengstorf, *art cit*, 423, to refer
'apostle' back to the theme of God's self-revelation in Christ in
1:2.

with some reluctance, aware of their distinctiveness, most clearly seen in their lack of anything that was recognisably temple, altar, priesthood or sacrifice. Hence the accusation, during the time of the imperial persecutions, that christians were atheists. Is it not, therefore, more probable that Hebrews' brilliant interpretation of the work of Christ in terms of priesthood, an interpretation now forever embodied in the New Testament revelation itself, is a piece of theological invention and apologia to meet just such a situation?[15]

Temple, altar, priesthood and sacrifice are all spiritualised in the New Testament.[16] In this connection the passage on 'God's house' in 3 : 2–6 is of in-

[15] C. F. D. Moule, in his article 'Sanctuary and sacrifice in the church of the New Testament', in *Journal of Theological Studies*, new series (1950), 29–55, shows the working of this apologia through many other passages of the New Testament apart from Hebrews. For Moule the whole theme of spiritual worship (*logikē latreia* Rm 12 : 1), and spiritual sacrifice (*pneumatikas thusias* 1 Pet 2 : 5), which he takes to be metaphorically worship and sacrifice, as also the conception of the believer and the christian community as the temple of the Spirit (1 Cor 6 : 19 and 3 : 16), are related to this apologia.

[16] In addition to the article by Moule referred to in the last footnote, see especially the article by M. Fraeyman, 'La spiritualisation de l'idée du Temple dans les épîtres pauliniennes', in *Ephemerides Theologiae Lovanienses* XXIII (1947), 378–412, which is written in criticism of the classical study by H. Wenschkewitz. 'Die Spiritualisierung der Kultusbegriffe Tempel, Priester und Opfer im Neuen Testament', in *Angelos* IV, 4 (1932), 71–230; and also A. Romeo in the two chapters 'La spiritualizzazione del culto' and 'Il sacerdozio di Gesù Cristo' in *Enciclopedia del sacerdozio*, ed G. Cacciatore, Florence 1953, 499–529.

terest. We may leave aside the difficulties that have been felt over fitting 3 : 4 into the argument, so that it has been regarded as a parenthesis (by eg Moffatt, Spicq, RSV) or 4b as a gloss (Héring), and by Vanhoye as the vital link in the argument. The house of God in which Moses was faithful was surely the Old Testament people of God (so Bruce and Héring; Vanhoye thinks that the house was equivalent to 'all things' (3 : 4)), the house of God over which Christ is faithful is we, the New Testament people of God. The 'house of God' here is surely not God's 'household' (Bruce), one does not build (*kataskeuazō*) a household; the house of God is rather the tent (temple) spiritualised as the people of God.[17]

The second section of the second part runs from 4 : 15 to 5 : 10, and the subject is that of the mercy of the high priest. This stands out very clearly in the first two verses of this section: 'For we have not a high priest who is unable to sympathise with our weaknesses, but one who in every respect has been

---

[17] Héring, *comm in loc*: 'God's house is constituted not only by the Tent, but also by the old covenant community.' The substitution of 'household' for 'house' obscures the wordplay on 'house' ie building and 'house' ie family, as in 1 Chr 17 : 10–14. Vanhoye, in his article 'Jesus "fidelis ei qui fecit eum" Heb 3 : 2', *Verbum Domini* XLV (1967), 302, finds this text from Chronicles, and to a lesser extent 1 Sa 2 : 35, latent in Heb 3 : 2. He thinks Moses a particularly apt 'type' for Jesus since Moses is regarded as a priest in later jewish tradition, Ps 99 : 6 and Philo, *De vita Moysis* II, 292. He admits, however, that Hebrews avoids directly calling Moses a priest.

tempted as we are, yet without sinning. Let us then with confidence draw near to the throne of grace, that we may receive mercy and find grace to help in time of need.'[18] This is important for a due appreciation of the description of high priesthood given in 5 : 1–4. This is in a context of preparation for the exposition of the high priesthood theme proper and 5 : 2 is explicable only in terms of its context: the high priesthood is being made like to Christ the merciful high priest. The quality of mercy hardly stands out from the Old Testament descriptions of the high priesthood[19] nor from the actual history of the Hasmonean high priests and their successors.[20] The elements of the description are, therefore,

[18] C. Bourgin, in his article 'Le Christ-prêtre et la purification des péchés selon l'Epître aux Hébreux', *Lumière et Vie* xxxvi (1958), 67–90, has remarked that the verb to 'draw near' (*proserchomai*), which is used of christians in 4 : 16, 7 : 25, 10 : 22, cf 7 : 19 (RSV 'draw near', Greek *engizō*), is a technical term in the LXX for priests 'drawing near' to the altar, eg Lv 9 : 7–8. Hebrews avoids using the word 'priest' of christians, in order to allow the priestly work of Christ to stand out in its stark uniqueness. The theme is hinted at in these passages, as also, in a different way, in 12 : 28 and 13 : 15–16. It is only through Christ that we are enabled to draw near to God 7 : 25. Spicq's commentary on 4 : 16 is also helpful.

[19] Bruce instances Aaron, and refers to Nm 14 : 5; 16 : 22, 47f; Ps 106 : 16. Only Nm 16 is really relevant; and since Aaron's 'mercy' consists in not wishing the entire people to be destroyed because of the sin of a few, in accordance with the old, primitive idea of collective solidarity in guilt (corrected in Ez 18; cf Jer 31 : 29–30), the observation in the text may stand.

[20] The commentators, eg Spicq and Bruce, remark upon the historical inaccuracy of the description.

chosen with an eye to their application to Christ.
'Gifts and sacrifices' sum up the whole of the Old
Testament sacrificial system, they are all regarded in
Hebrews as being made 'for sins' (5:1), even the
covenant sacrifice itself (9:18, 22). From a comparison of the description of the Old Testament
high priesthood with the application to Christ three
elements stand out on either side, arranged in an
order of concentric symmetry. Aaron was called by
God (5:4); Christ was exalted by God (5:5). (These
verses contain the priestly pair 'glory'—'exalt' is
doxazō—and honour—*timē* from 2:7 and 9.) The
high priest carried out his priestly work in compas-
sion and shared weakness (5:1b–3); Christ offered
up prayers and supplications in the weakness of
tears, fear of death, and suffering (5:7–8). The high
priest was taken from among men and appointed to
act on behalf of men (5:1); Christ became the source
of eternal salvation to all who obey him (5:9–10).[21]

In speaking of Christ's exaltation two psalm texts
are quoted. Commentators often suppose that the
first provides the theological foundation for the
priesthood of Christ; he is constituted a priestly
mediator between God and men by the very fact
of the incarnation.[22] Vanhoye rightly queries this

[21] Vanhoye, 110–111.
[22] Vanhoye, 112, n 1 cites Westcott, Moffatt, Riggenbach,
Médebielle, Bonsirven and Spicq. Héring and Bruce simply place
sonship and priesthood side by side without suggesting any
relationship of principle or cause between the two.

interpretation, and suggests that if we take the conjunction 'as . . . also' (*kathōs kai* of 5 : 6 as meaning 'according to what' (*selon que*) or 'for' (*etenim*) we will see that the second quotation does not merely complete the first; rather, the first merely prepares the way for the second, which alone provides the argument, the proof-text.[23] This is *the* proof-text of Hebrews, cited here to provide the basis for the great third part of the epistle which is concerned directly with the theme of priesthood, and in particular to provide the basis for the Melchizedek typology in chapter 7.

The sonship of Christ is already familiar to the Hebrews as to the earthly christians generally, and the use of Ps 2 : 7 and 110 : 1, as in 1 : 5 and 1 : 13, as proof-texts to establish this was likewise well known. In introducing his new theme (Vanhoye: 'the great revelation') of the priesthood of Christ, the author prepares the way by appealing to what is familiar. If Ps 2 : 7 and 110 : 1 find their fulfilment in Christ may this not also be true of 110 : 4? This way of reading the passage leaves the question of when Jesus became high priest, and still more when he

[23] Vanhoye, 112–113. In his footnote he refers to F. Zorell, *Lexicon Graecum NT*, at the word *kathōs*: 'Saepe indicatur conformitas rei gestae cum vaticinio, mandato, etc ubi *kathōs*: interdum argumentative—"etenim" . . .' The Blass-Debrunner-Funk *A Greek Grammar of the New Testament*, n 453 states: '(2) *hōs* and especially *kathōs* used to introduce a sentence may have something of the meaning "because" '.

began to act as high priest, completely open. We shall have reason, later, to think of Jesus as exercising his high priesthood precisely in the moment of his passion and death. The use of the verb 'exalt' ('glorify') here, and the puzzles that commentators have raised over the causal and temporal relationship between the earthly shedding of blood and the heavenly liturgy of atonement may suggest, as we shall see, that Hebrews, like the fourth gospel, thinks of the passion as coinciding with the glorification.

The parallel between the high priest offering gifts and sacrifices for sins and Christ offering prayers and supplications, with a loud cry and tears, to him who was able to save him from death, has puzzled commentators. Bruce, for example, rejects any sacrificial meaning in the word 'offer' (*prosphero*) in 5:7 'as though Christ's Gethsemane experience were somehow the counterpart to the Aaronic high priest's offering for himself in verse 3'. Yet Vanhoye's literary analysis establishes the counterpart beyond question. Others find the reference to Gethsemane a difficulty: since it is Christ's literal death that provides the literal New Testament sacrifice why do we not read about the death here? And was he heard for his godly fear (*eulabeia*) or heard and rescued from his fear (again *eulabeia*) of death?

The reference to Gethsemane seems to be well founded, whether one takes the second reading of *eulabeia* above or not, in the prayer to him who was

able to save him from death. But do we need to
choose between Gethsemane and Calvary? We have
already remarked the tendency of Hebrews to combine different incidents together into one; are not
Gethsemane and Calvary, the whole passion and
death of Christ evoked here? If the prayer for rescue
points especially to Gethsemane, does not the loud
cry (RSV, incorrectly, 'loud cries') point to Calvary,
either to the cry 'My God, My God, why hast thou
forsaken me?', Mk 15:34, or to the loud cry with
which Jesus died, Mk 15:37, or possibly to the two
taken as one? And if we forget, for the moment, in
the face of the passion narrative, our too clear and
distinct theological division between the death of
the body and the death of the soul, and remember
that death is a fearsome power over man, of darkness and estrangement from God, while the soul is
life, our living selves, as the psalms and the gospels
show, is not the cry of Mk 15:34 a prayer and sup-
plication to him who was able to save him from
death? If the prayer in Gethsemane and on the cross
are stressed here it is to emphasise that Christ's
'priesthood' was constituted by his obedience:
'Although he was a Son, he learned obedience
through what he suffered; and being made perfect'
was 'designated by God a high priest after the order
of Melchizedek' (5:8-10).

We have seen that 5:9-10 announce the themes
of the three sections of the third part of the epistle:

high priest according to the order of Melchizedek
5 : 10 and 6 : 20, theme of chapter 7; being made perfect 5 : 9 and 7 : 28, theme of 8 : 1–9 : 28; and source
of eternal salvation 5 : 9 (9 : 28 'unto salvation' ASV
of 1910; Greek *eis sōtērian*), the theme of 10 : 1–18.
Let us now turn to the third part.

Third part: Christ the high priest made perfect and source of eternal salvation, 5:11–10:39

We can omit, for our purposes, the introductory exhortation which opens the third part, 5 : 11–6 : 20,
noting only the evocation of the imagery of the tent
in 6 : 19–20: 'We have this (hope) as a sure and stead-
fast anchor of the soul, a hope that enters into the
inner shrine behind the curtain, where Jesus has
gone as a forerunner on our behalf, having become
a high priest for ever after the order of Melchizedek.'
The symbolism of the tent and of the liturgy of the
day of atonement will be fully exploited in chapter
9; in 10 : 20 the curtain is identified with the flesh
of Christ.

First section: high priest after the order of Melchizedek, 7:1–28

The seventh chapter falls into two unequal parts,
the first (7 : 1–10) concerned with Melchizedek and
the relation of his priesthood to the aaronite priesthood; the second (7 : 11–28) to the contrast between

the aaronite priesthood and the Melchizedek priesthood.[24]

We have already seen that in the description of Melchizedek he is made like to the Son of God (7:3) through the use of the principle: 'What is not spoken of in the law may be taken not to exist', so that we read of him: 'He is without father or mother or genealogy, and has neither beginning of days nor end of life, but resembling (being made like: *aphōmoiōmenos*) the Son of God he continues a priest for ever'. The theme of unending life is, of course, taken from Ps 110:4, where it belongs to the court style of davidic Jerusalem, as a comparison with Bathsheba's word to David, shortly before his death, 'May my lord King David live for ever' (1 Kgs 1:31), and that of the royal psalm quoted in Heb 1:8: 'Thy throne, O God, is for ever and ever' will show. Here, however, the phrase is taken literally of eternal life and is first, and artificially, read back into Genesis in order that it may then be taken up and applied typologically to the new priest after the order of Melchizedek. For Jesus has become a priest 'by the power of an indestructible life' (7:16), 'he holds his priesthood permanently, because he continues for ever' (7:24), 'he always lives to make intercession' (7:25), he offered himself 'through the

[24] Vanhoye, 125, points out an inclusion between 7:1 and 7:10 on the name 'Melchizedek' and the verb 'met', and between 7:11 and 7:28 on the words 'perfection' and 'made perfect'.

eternal Spirit' (9 : 14), our Lord Jesus has been brought back again from the dead (13 : 20), 'Jesus Christ is the same yesterday and today and for ever' (13 : 8). Belief in the eternal life of Jesus rests upon belief in the resurrection and in the divinity of Jesus; but for this belief Hebrews seeks a proof in the text of Genesis interpreted 'allegorically'.

There are two other elements in the text of Genesis exploited by Hebrews, the titles of Melchizedek and his reception of the tithes. The christological application of the two titles of Melchizedek 'king of righteousness' and 'king of peace' has been stressed by Spicq.[25] I suggest that these titles are in the author's mind at 7 : 25–26 where we read first that Jesus 'is able for all time to save those who draw near to God through him' and then that our high priest is 'holy, blameless, unstained, separated from sinners'. Reconciliation with God and with one another is precisely the peace of Christ: 'And he came and preached peace to you who were far off and peace to those who were near; for through him we both have access in one Spirit to the Father' (Eph 2 : 17–18). Jesus is separated from sinners because he has offered his sacrifice once for all for the sins of the people (7 : 27); he is the just servant of God and the source of justice for others ('the spirits of just men made

---

[25] Spicq, *comm in loc.*

perfect' (12 : 23)). He is king of our peace and king of our righteousness.[26]

The other element yet to be discussed is Melchizedek's receiving a tenth part of the booty from Abraham's successful reprisal raid. Hebrews is not concerned with the Abraham story for its own sake, but only with regard to the relationship between Melchizedek and Levi, which is, typologically, the relationship between Christ and the levitical priesthood. Hebrews stresses, therefore, the fact that Abraham the great patriarch gave tithes to Melchizedek and was blessed by him. By stretching the text to its ('allegorical') limit (*hōs epos eipein*: one might even say), Hebrews has Levi himself pay tithes to Melchizedek, 'for he was still in the loins of his ancestor when Melchizedek met him' (7 : 10).

Hebrews then turns to the application of Ps 110 : 4 to Jesus. First the incapacity of the levitical priesthood to reach or mediate perfection is stressed: this emerges from the very fact that another priest after the order of Melchizedek is spoken of at all in the psalm. The old justification for the taking over of the priestly functions of the Jebusite kings is turned into a proof of the total ineffectiveness of the levitical priesthood to bring about any improvement in men's

---

[26] This link between the christological titles and 7 : 25–26, if it is well founded, would not be mentioned by Vanhoye because it does not rest upon verbal stylistic indications but upon the conceptual meaning of the words.

moral standing before God. Nor is that all, the incapacity of the priesthood is the incapacity of the law itself 'for under it the people received the law' (7:11). This is to go much further even than the clericalising priestly editor of the pentateuch himself. The balance of the pentateuch is fundamentally altered by the insertion of the priestly texts, but the old texts are respected in their integrity. A reading of the old accounts of the receiving of the law and the covenant-making in Exodus will fail to reveal any such dependence of the law upon the priesthood.[27] Hebrews, however, is not concerned with the meaning of the law in itself, and for its own time and situation, but with the inefficacy of the law compared with the saving power of Christ. It is impossible that the priesthood of Christ should replace the levitical priesthood and yet remain within the confines of the law; there is, therefore, a change (removal: *metathesis*) of law as well as of priesthood.

The word 'change' or 'removal' occurs again at 12:27 in the context of the final eschatological shaking of heaven and earth when only God's unshakeable kingdom, which we have received, will survive. A comparison between the two texts suggests that it

---

[27] It is true that the priests were, at least at one time, the guardians and teachers of the law, Dt 33:10, but this means that the priests were servants of the law. See also Jer 2:8; Hos 4:6; Mal 2:7; referred to by Vanhoye in his article 'Jesus "fidelis ei qui fecit eum" Heb 3:20', in *Verbum Domini* xlv (1967), 291–305, at p 229.

is through the work of Christ priest and king that we have received the kingdom, and that the removal of the old priesthood and law is itself an eschatological event.

That there has been a change of priesthood is confirmed by the fact that our Lord belongs to the tribe of Judah, not of Levi. Because Jesus is that son of David, and therefore of Judah, of whom Ps 110:4 spoke, it is clear that the levitical priesthood has, in principle, been removed. Verse 15 therefore goes on immediately to echo the psalm: 'this becomes even more evident when another priest arises in the likeness of Melchizedek . . .'. In 7:19 the psalm verse is fully quoted, and Hebrews contrasts the weakness and uselessness of the commandment concerning priesthood and the imperfection of the law with the new and better hope through which we draw near to God. There is a further sign of the pre-eminence of Christ: the levitical priests were ordained without an oath, but this one, and here the psalm is quoted for the last time (though the 'for ever' continues to echo at 7:24 and 7:28), 'was addressed with an oath, "The Lord has sworn and will not change his mind: Thou art a priest for ever" '. The levitical priests were many since they had to succeed one another, but Jesus remains as priest for ever, he always lives to intercede for us (7:23–25).[28] Finally, the law

---

[28] Many authors have taken this statement concerning the heavenly intercession of Jesus as a proof for them, not only for

appointed sinful men in their weakness as high priests, but Jesus is sinless and has no need to offer sacrifice for his own sins; by the word of the oath which supersedes the law the holy Son of God, made perfect for ever, is appointed as priest (7 : 26–28). In this way the whole typology of chapter 7 is based upon the re-reading of Ps 110.[29]

---

the author of Hebrews, of his high priesthood, eg Cullmann, *The Christology of the New Testament*, Eng tr, London 1959, 102, 'a genuine high-priestly act'; A. J. B. Higgins, 'The Priestly Messiah', in *New Testament Studies* XIII (1967), 236, 'a priestly function performed by the exalted Jesus himself'; F. F. Bruce, *comm in loc*. Bruce first states 'here his high priestly function is summed up in terms of intercession', and then makes a comparison with Rm 8 : 33f, of which he says 'In these words we may trace the echo of an early christian confession of faith, which in addition to acknowledging the death, resurrection and enthronement of Christ makes mention also of his intercessory ministry.' This interpretation of the tradition of Jesus' intercession seems to forget that intercession is more especially a prophetic function in the Old Testament, eg Abraham's bargaining with God over Sodom in Gn 18 : 16–33, Moses' frequent intercessions for the people, eg Ex 32 : 7–14, and Jeremiah's prayers for the people, Jer 11 : 14; 15 : 11; 18 : 20. Prayer and intercession are also priestly functions, as in Hebrews, but a literal argument may not be constructed that leads from intercession to a deduction of priesthood.

[29] W. H. Brownlee, in his article 'Messianic motifs of Qumran and the New Testament', in *New Testament Studies* III (1957), 198, quotes a rabbinic text in which Ps 110:4 is used to establish the pre-eminence of the royal messiah over the priestly messiah: 'In Aboth de R. Nathan A, chapter 34, one reads the following comment upon Zech 4 : 15: "These are the two anointed ones (literally, sons of oil)." This means the Righteous Priest and the Messiah. And I do not know which of them is the more beloved. But since it says (Ps 110:4), "The Lord hath sworn and will not

Second section: having been made perfect, 8:1–9:28

With chapter 8 we begin the central section of the central part of the epistle. The theme of perfection which has already been announced in 5:9 is recalled again in the very last word of 7:28: *teteleiōmenon* 'made perfect'. Nor is this the only link between 7 and 8–9: chapter 7 establishes the superiority of Melchizedek's priesthood over the levitical priesthood and therefore the superiority of the new Melchizedek priesthood 'prophesied' in Ps 110:4; chapters 8 and 9 are concerned to establish the superiority of the new priesthood over the levitical priesthood and the superiority of the new covenant over the old. Naturally therefore a number of themes reappear: the daily sacrifices of the high priests[30] (7:27) and

---

repent: Thou art a priest for ever (after the order of Melchizedek)", we know that the King Messiah is more beloved than the Righteous Priest.' In this very interesting text we are an infinite distance away from the transcendent royal priesthood of Christ in Hebrews: Christ has no need of a righteous priest alongside him to supplement his work, for he is king, priest, and above all Son.

[30] No daily sacrifice for sin is prescribed in the old texts, only the annual atonement sacrifice (Lv 16:6), and a sacrifice for those occasions upon which a priest fell into 'sin' unwittingly (Lv 4:3). Nor were the daily sacrifices originally 'for sin' or part of the high priest's own liturgy (Nm 28:1–8; Ex 29:38–42). There is evidence, however, that the high priest offered the daily sacrifice at a later period (Ecclus 45:17) (cf Philo *Special Laws* 3, 131). For all this see the commentators, eg Spicq, Héring, Bruce, on 7:27. Since Hebrews seems to regard the old covenant sacrifice itself (Sinai) as a sacrifice for sin (9:18–22), the author does not hesitate to regard the daily sacrifices as sacrifices for sin. For him

the once yearly liturgy of the day of atonement (9:7, 25) ('repeatedly ... yearly') are contrasted with the once for all (*ephapax*) offering up of Christ himself (7:27) and his appearance once (*hapax*) for sacrifice (9:26) and offering (9:28). The high priest had 'to offer sacrifices first for his own sins and then for those of the people' (7:27) and in 9:7 he enters the second tent (ie the holy of holies) 'not without taking blood which he offers for himself and for the errors of the people'; in contrast Christ 'did this (ie offer for the sins of the people, cf 4:15) once for all when he offered up himself' (7:27) and 'appeared once for all at the end of the age to put away sin by the sacrifice of himself' (9:27).[31] To these more formal, literary parallels we may add the very important conceptual parallel between old law and new covenant. In Ex 24:7 the law of Ex 20–23 is identified with the book of the covenant; it is logical therefore that after hearing that 'when there is a change in the priesthood, there is necessarily a change in the law as well' (7:12), we should learn that Jesus is 'the surety of a better covenant' (7:22), and that 8:6–13 and 9:15–

---

the whole of the old sacrificial cultus, 'gifts and sacrifices' (9:9), is a vain endeavour to gain forgiveness of sins: 'according to this arrangement, gifts and sacrifices are offered which cannot perfect the conscience of the worshipper' (9:9). This rather arbitrary treatment of the Old Testament texts is yet another example of 'allegorical' procedures; the 'antitype' (9:24) has to be adapted for its application, by way of contrast, to the type.

[31] Vanhoye, 159–160.

4+

23 should develop the theme of the new covenant at length.[32]

The inner structure of chapters 8–9 is a very elaborate one; Vanhoye states that this is the most carefully developed part of the epistle and that there are far more indications of literary structure found here than elsewhere. A few of the principal indications of structure will suffice for our purpose here. At 8:3 we are told that every high priest is appointed to offer (*prospherō*) gifts and sacrifices, at 9:9 that 'gifts and sacrifices are offered (*prospherō* in the passive)'; in contrast, in 9:14 we read that Christ 'offered (*prospherō* in the perfect) himself without blemish to God' and in 9:25 'to offer (*prospherō*) himself' and in 9:28 'Christ, having been offered (*prospherō* in the perfect passive) once'. This shows that there are two main subdivisions, one concerned principally with the animal sacrifices of the Old Testament, the other with the self-offering of Christ. When the inclusion on the words 'regulations' (*dikaiōmata* 9:1 10) and 'worship' (*latreia* in 9:1 and *latreuonta* in 9:9) is taken together with the inclusion on the name 'Christ' in 9:11, 14, it is clear that the subdivisions are 8:1–9:10 and 9:11–9:28.

Each subdivision is then shown to be tripartite in

[32] The occurrence of 'covenant' at 7:22; 8:6, 13; 9:15 is, of course, a formal literary link. But it is important to see how the whole complexus of law, priesthood and covenant are contrasted with the work of Christ in 9:10.

structure. Working outwards from the centre 8:7 and 13 have an inclusion on 'first' (*prōtē:* the RSV supplies 'covenant' in each case) while 9:15–23 is built up out of two inner sections: 9:15–17 with an inclusion on 'covenant' (*diathēkē*) and 'made-a-covenant' (*diathemenos*), and 9:18–23 with an inclusion on 'blood' (*haima* and *haimatekchusia*) in 18 and 22.[33] Finally 8:1–6 has an inclusion on 'minister' (*leitourgos* 8:2) and 'ministry' (*leitourgia* 8:6); and 9:24–28 has an inclusion on the name 'Christ'.[34] The subdivisions correspond from the centre outwards: 9:1–10 speaks of the liturgy of the tent, 9:11–14 of Christ's liturgy in the 'holy place' which is entered through the 'tent not made with hands'; 8:7–13 is concerned with Jeremiah's prophecy of the new covenant; 9:15–23 with Christ's mediation of the new covenant in his death; 8:1–6 with the earthly liturgy of the levitical priests as contrasted with Christ's heavenly liturgy; 9:24–28 with Christ's heavenly liturgy.[35]

[33] That 9:23 belongs with 9:15–22 is shown by the repetition of 'necessary' (*anankē*) from 9:16 (RSV 'must'), and of 'purify' (*katharizō*) from 9:22; see Vanhoye, 152.

[34] The importance of the inclusions on the name 'Christ' stand out with greater clarity if one notices that the name 'Christ' and the name 'Jesus' are carefully avoided in the first subdivision, 8:1–9, 10 (the translations obscure this by adding the names, eg RSV). Vanhoye remarks that the epistle to the Hebrews is literally and literarily christocentric, pp 237–238.

[35] For the literary structure of chapters 8–9 see Vanhoye, 138–161.

Chapter 8 begins by emphasising the main point of the whole epistle: 'we have such a high priest, one who is seated at the right hand of the throne of the majesty in heaven . . .', a phrase which clearly looks right back to 1 : 3. We have arrived at the central section of the central part. Heb 8 : 1–6, as we have seen, is concerned with the earthly liturgy of the levitical priests in contrast with the heavenly liturgy of Christ our high priest. This contrast has often led commentators to think of Hebrews as a fundamentally hellenistic, indeed platonic, work in which the earthly Old Testament liturgy, precisely because earthly, could never be more than the shadow (10 : 1) (compare the shadows on the wall of the cave of Plato's *Republic*) of the true heavenly liturgy (9 : 24). This interpretation has the most embarrassing consequence, as these commentators have been the first to acknowledge and try to avoid, that the death of Christ on the cross is not part of his priestly work at all: 'if he were on earth he would not be a priest at all' (8 : 4) and 'Christ has entered, not into a sanctuary made with hands, a copy of the true one, but into heaven itself, now to appear in the presence of God on our behalf'. Spicq, who thinks that the author of Hebrews is an Alexandrian and a student of Philo who has been converted to christianity,[36] sums up this platonic interpretation:

[36] Spicq in his commentary, I, 39–91, and also in his article 'Le Philonisme de l'Epître aux Hébreux', in *Revue Biblique* LIV (1949), 542–572.

'When an eternal sacrifice and liturgy are spoken of a worship in spirit and truth is meant. For Hebrews, the spiritual world is the real world, and sensible realities are only the copy and the shadow of it, and this real world is not only spiritual and divine, but also eternal, while the terrestrial world is not only a lower one, but also temporary and transitory.' Yet Spicq tries to avoid the conclusion from this by saying 'The death of Christ on Calvary had value only because this sacrifice was already heavenly, already offered before God.'[37]

[37] Spicq, the article 'Paul', in *Supplément au Dictionnaire de la Bible* VII, col 264. The last sentence is repeated from his commentary I, 315; cf I, 287, n 4: 'on the cross the high priest officiated simultaneously on earth and in the heavenly sanctuary'. Higgins, in his article 'The priestly Messiah' already cited, stresses the affinity of Hebrews with the Apocalypse, p 235, n 1, and thinks of a purely jewish conception of the heavenly sanctuary and liturgy. He is able, therefore, to go on to draw a sharp distinction between the earthly sacrifice and the heavenly intercession, and sees the temporal distinction between the two made at 10:12: 'But when he had offered for all time a single sacrifice for sins, he sat down at the right hand of God'. I think Higgins is right about the jewish nature of the heavenly sanctuary, and Spicq correct in his conception of the simultaneity of the earthly and heavenly event: there can hardly be events in a platonic heaven.

W. Stott, in his article 'The concept of "offering" in the Epistle to the Hebrews', *New Testament Studies* IX (1962), 62–67, has tried to show from Leviticus that the atonement sacrifice *is* the slaying of the bullock and the goat, that the high priest offers (*prosphero*; *hiqribh*) in slaying, and that the use of the blood is secondary, a matter of taking in (*laqah*), and of making to enter in (*hibhi*). From this he argues that the offering of Hebrews necessarily precedes the entry into the heavenly sanctuary.

A closer examination of Hebrews, whatever may be true of

This last statement is, I think, accurate, but it needs more evidential support than Spicq has been able to find for it. Though this will lead us to anticipate, some such evidence should be provided here.

A quite unnecessary difficulty has been raised by supplying the verb 'is' in 8:3: 'For every high priest is appointed to offer gifts and sacrifices; hence it is necessary for this priest also to have something to offer.' The second clause should begin 'hence the necessity'; the infinitive 'to offer' represents the Greek aorist subjunctive *ho prosenenkē* which cannot be rendered literally in English ('which he might offered'). The verb 'to offer' is used in the present of the Old Testament high priest at 8:3, 4 ('priests'), at 9:7, 25, and also at 10:1, 2; throughout the aorist is used of Christ's offering (7:27 (*anenenkas*); 8:3; 9:14; 9:28; 10:12).[38] The sacri-

---

Leviticus, will show that Hebrews regards the entry into the sanctuary with the blood as the 'offering': 'into the second (tent) only the high priest goes, and he but once a year, and not without taking blood which he offers for himself and for the errors of the people' (9:7). This is also the natural interpretation of the sequence in 9:24–25: 'For Christ has entered, not into a sanctuary made with hands, a copy of the true one, but into heaven itself, now to appear in the presence of God on our behalf. Nor was it to offer himself repeatedly, as the high priest enters into the Holy Place yearly with blood not his own...' There can be no doubt, therefore, that Hebrews thinks of a heavenly sacrifice which consists in the offering of the blood. The problem is to make sense of this without hedging.

[38] Bruce and Vanhoye have brought out this time element of the verbs, apparently independent of one another. See Bruce,

fice, the offering, of Christ is therefore a single unique event that may have, and indeed has, consequences for the whole of the future but is not 'eternal' in any platonic sense of the word.

To this evidence from time which suggests an earthly happening, rather than a platonically heavenly one, the evidence concerning the shedding or sprinkling of Christ's blood should be added (again by way of anticipation). In 9:12 it is stated that Christ entered into the holy place through his own blood, not that of goats and calves; in 9:14 that the blood of Christ purifies our conscience from dead works. In 9:25 we are told of Christ's entry into heaven: 'Nor was it to offer himself repeatedly, as the high priest enters the Holy Place yearly with blood not his own. . . .' In 10:19 we read 'we have confidence to enter the sanctuary by the blood of Jesus . . .', which in 10:29 is the blood of the covenant by which we have been sanctified. In 12:24 we learn that we have come 'to Jesus, the mediator of a new covenant, and to the sprinkled blood that speaks more graciously than the blood of Abel'; at 13:12

---

comm in loc (8:3) with the notes 20 and 21. Vanhoye is more thorough, and points out that it would be wrong even to supply 'was' instead of 'is', as Bruce suggests (NEB footnote 'this one too must have had something to offer'), since the copula is deliberately omitted here in what is merely a preparatory passage. It is in 9:24-28 that the author's meaning is to be sought. See Vanhoye, 'De "aspectu" oblationis secundum Epistulam ad Hebraeos', *Verbum Domini* XXXVII (1959), 32-39.

'So Jesus also suffered outside the gate in order to sanctify the people through his own blood'.

In order that the symbolism of the day of atonement might be apt for the description of the work of Christ these quotations are strictly compatible with a death on the cross, complete with the shedding of blood, followed by the entry (after resurrection?) into the heavenly holy place there to sprinkle the blood before God. But does not such an interpretation, taken with any kind of literalness, neglect a number of other indications in the text? For, in the first place, there is no explicit reference to the ascension at all, and the resurrection is spoken of only in the conclusion of the epistle, surely a very deliberate restraint on the part of so careful and disciplined a writer: 'Now may the God of peace who brought again from the dead our Lord Jesus, the great shepherd of the sheep, by the blood of the eternal covenant...' (13:20). It is by the blood of the eternal covenant that Jesus is brought again from the dead, and yet in 9:18–24 the blood ritual of Jesus' covenant-making is carried out in heaven. The parallelism between the blood of Abel: 'And the Lord said: What have you done? The voice of your brother's blood is crying to me from the ground' (Gn 4:10), and the blood of Christ strongly suggests that Jesus' blood was sprinkled on the ground of Calvary and simultaneously in God's sight 'in heaven', 'outside the gate' (of the earthly Jerusalem) as 13:12 states, yet at the same time in 'Mount Zion . . . the city of the living God, the heavenly Jerusalem' (12 : 22) (the sprinkled blood is spoken of at the end of the same sentence).

With these converging lines of proof laid down, Spicq's intuition would appear well justified. One may sum up the position in Vanhoye's words:

> All the indications that we have found converge upon one point: when the author of Hebrews speaks of Christ's offering he is not thinking of any continuing heavenly liturgy, nor, directly, of the internal dispositions of the incarnate Word, but rather of one determinate and decisive event, which was indeed at once heavenly and earthly, internal and manifest, but nevertheless a unique historical event.[39]

With these general considerations about earthly and heavenly, historical and eternal, in mind, we may return to 8 : 1–6. C. F. D. Moule has pointed out the parallel between 8 : 1 'we have such a high priest' and 13 : 10 'We have an altar' and comments 'the whole burden of the Epistle can, accordingly, be epitomised in two resounding *echomens*: we *have* a high priest, we *have* an altar: sacrifice and sanctuary are ours'. Moule sees these texts, and the many New Testament texts which speak of spiritual worship and spiritual sacrifice, in terms of a 'no-sacrifice

---

[39] Vanhoye, *art cit*, 39.

4*

apologia' on the part of the early church, a self-justi-
fication in the face of accusations of irreligion and
atheism. A fuller discussion of this point may be left
till we come to 9 : 14.[40]

In 8 : 2 we read that our high priest is 'a minister
in the sanctuary and the true tent which is set up
not by man but by the Lord'. The true tent here is
the 'greater and more perfect tent not made with
hands, that is, not of this creation' of 9 : 11, which
is in parallel with Christ's blood in 9 : 12 and is to
be identified with the (risen) body of Christ, as we
shall see. In 9 : 24 we read 'Christ has entered, not
into a sanctuary made with hands, a copy of the true
one, but into heaven itself, now to appear in the
presence of God on our behalf'. In 10 : 19–21 Jesus
is at once the great priest over the house of God,
while his flesh is the curtain before the sanctuary,
and his blood, by which we enter, has opened (dedi-
cated: *enkainizō*) the new and living way through
for us. It is obvious that Hebrews is not concerned
with preserving any precise, spatial image of the
'geography' of the heavenly sanctuary. Indeed the
occurrence of 'sanctuary' (*ta hagia*: which is distin-
guished from the inner shrine (the most holy tent:
skēnē . . . hagia hagiōn) only at 9 : 2–3, and elsewhere,
eg 9 : 25, clearly indicates the inner shrine) in
parallel with 'true tent' in 8 : 2, strongly suggests

---

[40] Moule, *art cit*, 37.

that the risen body of Christ is the heavenly holy place in which God dwells.[41]

The meaning of 'true' here has clear affinities with the johannine use of 'true', and particularly where it is combined with metaphor as in the phrase 'the true light' and 'the true vine' (Jn 1 : 9 and 15 : 1). It means not so much 'true' as distinct from 'false', as 'true', 'real', 'authentic', 'divine' in contrast with the transitoriness of earthly realities which do, nevertheless, themselves come from the hand of God. This sense of 'true' is compatible with metaphor since the reality towards which the imagery points partakes of the reality of God. The vine points to the unity of the church with Christ, and to the true, divine life that he communicates to his members: he, therefore, is the 'true vine'. The imagery of the temple points directly and naturally to the theme of access to God: Jesus is the 'true tent' since it is through his flesh (10 : 20) and blood (9 : 12) that we have access to the reality of God.[42]

[41] Héring, comm in loc, accepts the identification in 8 : 2, though he thinks that ta hagia there means both tents, ie the outer and inner sanctuaries.

[42] Héring makes the comparison with John, but claims that there is a great difference, since John contrasts true with false, Hebrews the original with the model in platonic fashion. R. Bultmann, in his article alētheia in TWNT I, 672, also makes the comparison with John but explains them both from a rather platonising starting-point. This is questionable, but his final account of the meaning of the word here and in John is accurate and helpful: authentic, ie divine. Bruce, who is in general suspicious of a platonising reading of Hebrews, and emphasises

'Now if he were on earth, he would not be a priest
at all, since there are priests who offer gifts according
to the law' (8:4). This is the clearest statement in
the whole of the New Testament, necessary only in
Hebrews which alone uses the word 'priest' of
Christ, that his priesthood is not of this world; the
parallel with Jn 18:36 'My kingship is not of this
world' is striking. Bruce comments upon the passage
in Hebrews: 'On earth Jesus was a layman, excluded
by the law from all priestly functions'. This is a perspective too often lost sight of when we look back
on the last supper from the apparent standpoint of
Hebrews. It is perhaps instructive to compare
Hebrews 'on earth' with St Paul's 'according to the
flesh' (*kata sarka*: RSV 'from a human point of view')
(2 Cor 5:16). It is in the light of the Easter faith
that Jesus is known to be Lord, and Lord even in
the moment of crucifixion: 'None of the rulers of
this age understood this; for if they had, they would
not have crucified the Lord of glory' (1 Cor 2:8). In
somewhat comparable fashion it is only in the light
of the resurrection and ascension that the death of

the similarities between Hebrews' idea of heaven and the completely jewish picture of the heavenly Jerusalem in the
Apocalypse, makes a reference to John here, and apparently
reads them both in a non-platonic way. Whatever direct or indirect influences there may be, it does not seem that the fundamental conceptions of either Hebrews or John are distinctively
platonic or hellenistic. The idea of the heavenly original for the
earthly temple is a commonplace of ancient Near-Eastern
thought.

Christ upon the cross can be seen to be the entry of the high priest into the heavenly holy place, that the blood shed upon the earth of Calvary is simultaneously sprinkled before God in heaven.

There is one last point to be considered before we leave 8:1–6: Christ's role as mediator (*mesitēs*) of the new covenant, which is the subject of the next sub-division, 8:7–13. The fact that Jesus is mediator between God and men, 'chosen from among men . . . in relation to God' (5:1), is often taken as proof or even as definition of his priesthood. Consider, for example, this statement by Oscar Cullmann: 'The term *mesitēs*, Mediator, a *terminus technicus* of legal language designating an arbitrator or guarantor, also appears in this letter (8:6; 9:15; 12:24) as well as in 1 Tm 2:5. Since it is only a variant of the concept High Priest, we need not devote a special chapter to it.' Whatever else the concept of high priest may be, it is certainly not merely a legal concept; and if a legal concept is stretched and broken so as to point to the same reality that the image 'high priest' points to, we may legitimately ask for some discrimination between starting point and the ultimate reality suggested in the image. Cullmann's two sentences above are mutually incoherent: the first refutes the second.[43]

[43] The quotation is from Cullmann's *The Christology of the New Testament*, Eng tr, London 1959, 89.

Turning now to the first passage on the new covenant, 8:7–13, it is not necessary to add much to what was said about the interpretation of Jeremiah's prophecy, and the transferred sense in which it is used by Hebrews, in the first chapter. It is true that 'if that first (covenant; supplied by RSV correctly according to the sense) had been faultless, there would have been no occasion for a second'. It was because the people had, as throughout their history, failed from their side to keep the covenant and obey the law that a renewal of covenant was necessary. But Hebrews goes further than that: the first covenant was itself not without fault since the people stood in need of redemption from the transgressions under the first covenant until the time of the death of Christ (9:15). Hebrews, though not, historically speaking, Jeremiah, regards the old covenant as obsolete, growing old, and ready to vanish away (8:13).

The passage on the tent and its liturgy (9:1–10) contains some curious features that have puzzled interpreters, eg the apparent placing of the altar of incense (if this is what *thumiatērion* means, the LXX use it for 'censer') inside the holy of holies. These points need not concern us. More interesting is the contrast between the continual ministry of the priests in the outer (literally 'first') tent and the high priest's going in 'once a year' (*hapax tou eniautou*) into the second, and not without taking blood. The high priest goes in only once a year, Jesus the high priest has entered 'once for all' (*ephapax*) into the holy place through (RSV 'taking') his own blood (9:12). Hebrews comments on these liturgical arrangements: 'By this the Holy Spirit indicates that the way into the sanctuary is not yet opened (Greek from *phaneroō* 'manifested') as long as the outer tent is still standing (which is symbolic for the present age).' The word 'symbolic' is literally 'a parable' (*parabolē*). Spicq quotes Chrysostom, Oecumenius, Hervé de Bourg-Dieu, Westcott, Médebielle and Bonsirven as supporting an equivalence between 'parable' and 'type'. His own language is more general: 'a parable in act, that is to say an analogy, a parallel, or rather a symbol, a lesson'.[44] Hebrews' choice of word does indeed seem at once to acknowledge a certain value in the liturgical ritual of the Old Testament in its own time, though of course 'the law made nothing perfect' (7:19), and to find in it a lesson that the Holy Spirit wishes to teach us in our own situation. This would seem to be a 'typical sense' in the mediaeval meaning of the phrase, an 'allegorical', not a literal sense. 'The present age' is ambiguous, but would be more literally rendered 'the season that has begun to stand in (upon us)' in Greek *ton kairon ton enestēkota*; this would seem to be the time inaugurated by the death of Christ rather than the present evil aeon of the gospels and

[44] Spicq, *comm in loc.* Héring suggests 'typologically'; Bruce quotes W. Manson: 'a parable bearing on the present crisis'.

jewish apocalyptic which is contrasted with the aeon to come.[45]

Hebrews' further comment is of particular interest: 'According to this arrangement, gifts and sacrifices are offered which cannot perfect the conscience of the worshipper, but deal only with food and drink and various ablutions, regulations for the body imposed until the time of reformation' (9:9–10). The perfecting of the conscience of the worshipper is parallel to 9:14 'purify our (RSV 'your') conscience from dead works'; this shows that indeed Hebrews makes no distinction between 'gifts' and 'sacrifices' in relation to offerings for sin. The judgment of Hebrews upon Old Testament ritual, and above all that of the day of atonement, is a polemical christian evaluation rather than a careful historical exegesis of the old texts. Certainly jewish exegesis, without any apparent polemical intention and of a time fairly near to that of Hebrews, reads these texts in a quite different way. Consider this classic text concerning expiation on the day of atonement by Rabbi Ishmael, who died about the year 135 of the christian era:

> There are four kinds of expiation: he who breaks a positive commandment and does penance will certainly be forgiven, according to Jer 3:23; he

[45] Eg Mt 12:32. Héring suggests simply 'our time' for the phrase in Hebrews.

who breaks a negative commandment, if he does penance, remains in suspense till the day of atonement which makes expiation for him, according to Lv 16:30; he who breaks commandments involving extermination or death by court sentence, the day of atonement places him in suspension and his punishment makes expiation, according to Ps 89:33; but he who profanes the heavenly name, if he does penance, his penance cannot place him in suspension nor the day of atonement purify him, but his penance and the day of atonement expiate one third, the punishments endured during the rest of the year expiate one third, and the day of his death purifies him, according to Ex 23:21.[46]

This text shows no evident sign of a reaction to christian ideas or of an antichristian polemic; it seems that the jewish understanding of the propitiatory effectiveness of the liturgy of the day of atonement was entirely different from that of Hebrews. We have seen that Cambier, at least, regards the Old Testament sacrifices as effective in their own way

[46] Quoted from T. Yom Hakippurim v, 6–9, 190, as cited in J. Bonsirven. *Le Judaisme Palestinien au temps de Jésus Christ* II, Paris 1935, 92–93. Spicq refers to this quotation in Bonsirven, but in order to support a literal reading of Hebrews: even the rabbis admitted the deficiency of the expiation ritual of the day of atonement! This is to fail to see the wood for the trees. For a similar, though simpler, conception of suspension till the day of atonement through repentance see the Mishnah, Yoma 8:8.

with regard to man's moral (conscientious) standing before God. St Thomas' standpoint was naturally a rather different one, and his *sed contra*, his argument from the relevant theological *auctoritas*, in his article 'whether the sacraments of the old law cause grace?' in the *Summa Theologiae*, is firmly based upon pauline theology, upon the words from Gal 4 : 9: 'you turn back again to the weak and beggarly elemental spirits', which the *Glossa Ordinaria* interpreted as the law. Even within this perspective St Thomas was able to give a real value to the 'sacraments of the old law' as protestations of faith. Implicit in them is faith in the transforming power of the passion of Christ, and so the Old Testament liturgy was an occasion of grace precisely as a sign and protestation of faith which justifies.[47]

The paragraph 9 : 11–14 is the theological centre of Hebrews, as Vanhoye's inescapable analysis reveals this to us. The twin subdivisions, one concerned with Old Testament, one with New, that stand at the centre of the third and central section of the third and central part, run from 9 : 1–10 and 9 : 11–14. The first phrase presents a well-known textual difficulty: some manuscripts support the translation of the text of the RSV: 'But when Christ appeared as a high priest of the good things that have come', others the reading of the footnote 'good

---

[47] *Summa theologiae*, 3a. 62. 6.

things to come'.[48] The difference does not seem to be of any final importance: Christ is now high priest and has already secured eternal redemption (9:12), 'by a single offering he has perfected for all time those who are sanctified' (10:14). On the other hand, christians are those who 'have tasted the goodness of the word of God and the powers of the age to come' (6:5). Redemption and sanctification are surely the 'powers (*dunameis*: Bruce suggests "mighty works") of the age to come' which are nevertheless active within the christian community. Vanhoye's study of the structure of 9:11–12 discovers a concentric symmetry in which 'the good things to come' is parallel with 'eternal redemption'. The parallel would seem to demand the other (RSV) reading.[49] This is of some importance for the theme of the next chapter: the realised eschatology of Hebrews.

The literary analysis of 9:11–12 reveals another parallel that is relevant to the priestly imagery of

[48] Manuscript support for the reading with the future meaning (*mellontōn*) is numerically stronger: Sinaiticus, Alexandrinus, most of the Itala manuscripts, the Vulgate, the Coptic and a larger number of the fathers. On the other hand, the witnesses to the reading 'are come' (*genomenōn*) are particularly weighty: papyrus 46 (*genamenōn*), Vaticanus, the original reading of Claromontanus, two Itala manuscripts, the Syriac, and Origen among the fathers. *The Greek New Testament*, ed K. Aland, M. Black, B. M. Metzger and A. Wikgren, New York, London etc 1966, adopts the reading *genomenōn* but accords it only third-class certainty.

[49] Vanhoye, 149. On p 66, n 1, Vanhoye states that he follows the text of A. Merk, *Novum Testamentum*, 8th edn, Rome 1958, throughout, except for details in 9:2–3, 11:37 and 12:1.

Hebrews: that between 'through the greater . . . tent' and 'through (RSV 'taking', which, in the light of 9:7 and 25 I regard as correct so far as the meaning goes[50]) . . . his own blood', as also 'not made with hands' is parallel to 'not the blood of goats . . .'. The parallel between the tent and the blood strongly supports the interpretation of 'the greater and more perfect tent, not made with hands, that is, not of this creation' to mean the body of Christ or, as Vanhoye insists, the risen body of Christ.[51] I would suggest

[50] Bruce sternly criticises RSV for translating 'though' as 'taking'; but this is because he is thinking of interpreters who speak of Jesus completing his atoning work literally in heaven and not on the cross. If one thinks of Christ's death on the cross as simultaneously a heavenly and an earthly event, this objection falls away. One cannot but agree whole-heartedly with Bruce's comment on the consequences of the literalising exegesis: 'it serves only to warn those who require such a warning against basing doctrines on types, instead of using types to illustrate securely based doctrines' (201, n 82). There may be occasions on which a doctrine is given to us only in a typological text of scripture; the atonement of Christ on the cross is not one of these.

[51] Vanhoye, 157, n 1, compares this passage with Mk 14:58. He criticises Bonsirven (comm in loc) and A. Feuillet, 'La demeure celeste et la destinée des chrétiens', Récherches de Science Religieuse XLIV (1956), 160–192, 360–402, for not going far enough in speaking of 'the body of the Incarnate Word', since that body is part of the first creation until death. Moffatt, Spicq and Héring identify the tent with the heavens but, as Vanhoye points out, these are certainly part of the first creation. Vanhoye does not actually use the phrase 'the risen body' in his book, but that is certainly his meaning, see his article 'Par la tente plus grande et plus parfaite . . . Heb 9:11', in Biblica XLVI (1965), 1–28. J. Swetnam, in an article 'On the imagery and significance of Hebrews 9:9–10', in Catholic Biblical Quarterly XXVII (1966),

that as Christ's body dies on the cross, that unique event which is simultaneously earthly and heavenly, it is already sealed by God for resurrection. As Christ dies in his body to this sinful world his body is already, in God's sight, 'not of this creation'.[52] Nowhere in the New Testament is the uniqueness of the Christ event brought out with greater force than in Hebrews; but this does not imply an interest in all the details of time and place in the gospel story. We have seen that the resurrection is mentioned only in the conclusion of Hebrews, and then without any mention of the third day or the empty tomb. The ascension, or to use the word that occurs more frequently in the New Testament accounts, the assumption (eg Ac 1 : 11) of Jesus, whether on the fortieth day, as in Acts, or on the third, as apparently in the longer ending to Mark, in Luke and John, is not mentioned at all, though the entry into heaven (9 : 24), and the exaltation above the heavens

155–173, has tried to improve on Vanhoye by suggesting that it is the risen and eucharistic body and blood of Jesus that are meant. This strikes one as fanciful, and his arguments are hardly conclusive: he is very anxious to find references to the eucharist in various texts in Hebrews.

[52] Compare this statement of Spicq's concerning Christ's entry into heaven: 'It is not quite exact to identify, as people customarily do, this appearance before God with the Ascension, which is not explicitly mentioned in Hebrews. This entry into heaven should be identified rather with the Resurrection; or more probably still, on the Cross the high priest officiated simultaneously on earth and in the heavenly sanctuary...' *op cit* I, 287, n 4.

(7:26) are spoken of, and also the passing through
the heavens (4:14). We have already seen some evidence for the idea that the blood shed 'outside the
gate' (13:12) was simultaneously sprinkled in
heaven (12:24). Further, the parallel between 'not
made with hands, that is, not of this creation' with
'not the blood of goats and calves' is suggestive: goats
and calves (and most emphatically not human
beings) were the appropriate offerings on earth (8:4),
Christ's sacrificial body, like his priesthood (8:4), is
therefore a heavenly reality. I would suggest that
'heavenly' implies 'spiritual' (cf 9:14), and that
'spiritual' implies 'metaphorical' or, better, that it
is a biblical image. This we shall examine in relation to 9:14.

Before we leave 9:12 there are two points to be
made. First, the central statement of 9:11-12 is 'he
entered once for all into the Holy Place'. The emphasis of Hebrews on 'once' and 'once for all' will
be examined in the next chapter, here it will suffice
to note the strong contrast with the continual ministry of the priests and the high priest's annual entry
into the inner shrine in 9:6-7.[53] Secondly, the last
words of 9:12: 'thus securing (literally "finding") an
eternal redemption', introduces a new and slightly
extraneous element into the symbolism of the day
of atonement. For the biblical theme of redemption

[53] Vanhoye, 150.

is not, properly speaking, a sacrificial idea at all[54]; it is brought into a rather exterior relationship with sacrifice when there is question of 'redeeming' the first-born of asses or men (Ex 13:13). God's redemption of his people from Egypt is, however, one of the great themes of the Old Testament and stands behind the dominical saying of Mk 10:45 that is so often echoed in the New Testament: 'For the Son of Man also came not to be served but to serve, and to give his life as a ransom (ie a redemption price for slaves) for many.' It is surely from early christian tradition that the theme of redemption finds its way into Hebrews by way of reminder to us of the foundation upon which the symbolic structure of the epistle is built.[55]

Heb 9:13–14, the second half of our small subdivision, is constructed in parallel symmetry: 'the blood of goats and bulls' is parallel with 'the blood of Christ', 'the sprinkling of defiled persons' with

[54] The idea that redemption is a ritual and sacrificial concept is extraordinarily widespread; see, among recent writers, M. Barth, *Was Christ's death a sacrifice?*, Edinburgh 1961, 2, and Bruce, 201: 'The Aaronic high priests had to present themselves before God repeatedly, because such redemption as their ministry procured bore but a token and a temporary character...' Vanhoye, in his article previously quoted 'De Christologia...' very accurately and usefully excludes any properly ritual and sacrificial significance from such words and phrases as 'freeing, redeeming, buying, for sins, for us, for many'.

[55] M. Barth, 4, presents briefly the present state of scholarly opinion on the authenticity of the saying in Mk 10:45 and comes out in favour of accepting it.

'offered himself without blemish', and 'for the purification of the flesh' with 'shall . . . purify our (RSV "your" following other manuscripts; the divergence is not relevant to our theme) conscience'.[56] The parallel and contrast between the blood of goats and bulls, the appropriate offering upon earth, and the blood of Christ strongly suggests, once again, that the blood of Christ is heavenly in nature. This is confirmed by the phrase about Christ's self offering through the eternal Spirit. 'The sprinkling of defiled persons' is in strong contrast to the sinless 'unblemished' Christ, for the inner defilement of sin and transgression (9:15) remained, as the third contrast brings out: the Old Testament liturgy was effective only so far as the 'flesh' was concerned, the sacrifice of Christ is alone effective for the 'purification' of consciences.

There is a curious feature in the description of the Old Testament ritual that has often gone unremarked by commentators[57]: the sprinkling of the defiled persons with the blood of goats and bulls and with the ashes of a heifer. The blood of goats and bulls is used in sin offerings (Lv 4) and in the ritual of the day of atonement (Lv 16); but the blood is never sprinkled upon the defiled persons, it is sprinkled before the veil, put on the horns of the

[56] Vanhoye, 149. The parallel symmetry depends upon the order of the words in the Greek, where 'the blood of goats and bulls' is at the beginning of the verse.
[57] Eg Héring and Bruce, *ad loc.*

incense altar, poured out at the base of the altar for holocausts and, at atonement, before and upon the mercy seat that covers the ark. The ashes of the heifer, however, are mixed into the water for (the removal of) impurity with which any man rendered unclean by contact with the dead had to cleanse himself (Nm 17). The only ritual which speaks of the sprinkling of people with blood is the covenant-making ritual described in Ex 24 and Heb 9:18–20. Here, once again, we find Hebrews combining together rituals and events that were originally distinct in order that they may be typologically contrasted with the perfect sacrifice of Christ. This is one of the procedures that we may call 'allegorical' in the wide sense.

Vanhoye's analysis of the literary structure shows a parallel and contrast between 'the purification of the flesh' and 'purify our conscience'; there is another contrast later in these verses, the classic Old Testament contrast between 'flesh' and 'spirit', as, for example, in Is 31:1–3. Vanhoye points to the parallel and contrast between 'regulations of the flesh' (RSV 'body', inaccurately)' in 9:10 and 'through an eternal spirit' in 9:14. There is no trace of docetism in Hebrews, Jesus shares in flesh and blood (2:14) and it was in the days of his flesh that he offered up prayers and supplications (5:7); yet Jesus' flesh and blood is not mere flesh and blood since it is offered through the eternal Spirit. I have discussed earlier the different interpretations of 'spirit' here, either the 'power of an indestructible life' of 7:16 or the Holy Spirit spoken of in 9:8, and indicated that in any case I think the one connotes the other. In view of the proximity of 9:8 I am inclined to follow the RSV and take 'Spirit' as the direct meaning and 'spirit' as the connoted one.

There is general agreement among the commentators that the sacrifice of Christ, because it was offered through the eternal Spirit, was a spiritual sacrifice and the foundation upon which the spiritual sacrifice of christians rests (13:15–16). In 9:14 we are told that we are purified through the blood of Christ 'to serve (*latreuein*: to worship) the living (for God is Spirit) God'. But when one comes to search the commentators to find out what they mean by 'spiritual' one discovers a fundamental divergence of interpretation between those who think that Christ's sacrifice is spiritual in a quite different way from that in which praise, confession, doing good and sharing what one has are spiritual sacrifices (13:15–16) (Hebrews does not use the word 'spiritual' explicitly of those sacrifices but the parallel with 1 Pt 2:5, Rm 12:1 and Jn 4:23–24 is generally admitted), and those who think that the meaning is the same, granted an infinite or total diversity of value. The first interpretation is by no means confined to catholics, it is upheld also, for example, by Westcott among older writers, and more recently by Héring, M. Barth[58] and Bruce. All those authors, in fact, who interpret literally those passages in Hebrews which speak of Christ's priesthood and sacrifice fall within this group. The second group is represented by Moffatt among older writers, and by Schrenk, Moule and possibly Riesenfeld.[59]

[58] M. Barth, *Was Christ's death a sacrifice?*

[59] G. Schrenk, in his article *archiereus*, TWNT III, 275, speaks of the 'cultic metaphor' of Hebrews. Moule, *art cit*, establishes an equivalence between *logikos* (literally but misleadingly 'reasonable' (Rm 12:1), RSV 'spiritual', and *pneumatikos* (1 Pet 2:5). He suggests that 1 Pet 2:2 should be translated 'the *unadulterated spiritual* (that is *metaphorical*, not *literal*) *milk* upon which Christians are nourished', p 34. (The italics in the English words are Moule's.) On p 36 he writes: 'St Paul has come to take a certain delight also in "sublimating" the Levitical terms and Judaistic phrases, which had been his former boast, into purely spiritual senses, wholly on the level of personal relationships and volition, in which the supreme sacrifice (as in Hebrews) is the self-oblation of Christ ... and in this offering of Christ is involved also the self-oblation of christians. ...'

H. Riesenfeld speaks less clearly, but I think his concept of 'transformation' places him in this group. Consider this passage from his essay 'The mythical background of New Testament Christology' (the title is a significant one) published in *The background of the New Testament and its eschatology*, ed W. D. Davies and D. Daube, Cambridge 1956, 93: 'The third creative process, that of transformation, has operated upon all the motifs and elements which in the words of Jesus have been selected from Jewish eschatology and which, having been combined in a unique way, constitute the picture of Jesus the Christ which emerges from the pages of the New Testament. Here we still presuppose that Jesus himself was the author of this christological conception. Transformation is in reality the essence of the recreation which in New Testament terminology is called fulfilment. If we take the motif of kingship, we see in what a radical way it has been changed. Christ is really king in the fullest sense of the word, but apart from the nature of his

What is particularly striking is that the language used by the first, literal-minded, group often comes close to that used by members of the second. Let us take, for example, this passage from an article by A. Romeo:

> The true priesthood is the priesthood of Jesus, who came into the world for the single purpose of offering himself in sacrifice, obedient to the will of God in all his actions, even to the death on the cross (Phil 2:5–8). In this sacrifice of the Son of God made man is founded the sanctification of all men (Heb 10:5–10). The deeper meaning of sacrifice, wholly spiritualised and taken out of the area of a material and external (*sensibile*) worship, is realised only in Christ: for the first time on earth the will of God is fully carried out in a human life. The sacrifice of Christ, since it is the fulfilment, the total and final perfecting of the Hebrew religious and cultic establishment, abrogates it and empties it of meaning; it remains a moving and instructive reminder, but as a reality it is passed.

---

kingdom, his glory is the result not of his power but of his service. His victory is won not in a fight against nations or cosmic powers but by obedience and suffering. The priestly function of Christ is performed not in the temple of Jerusalem or in an ideal sanctuary of a similar kind but in the sacrifice of the cross, interpreted and communicated by the sacrament of the Last Supper.' The word 'really' in the phrase 'really king in the fullest sense of the word' seems to be the equivalent of the fourth gospel's 'true'.

And a few pages later:

> True sacrifice, the only one that has any value, is
> fulfilment of God's will. The fundamental prin-
> ciple that 'God prefers obedience to holocausts
> and sacrifices' (1 Sa 15:22 etc) is placed by Jesus
> at the very foundation of the new religious estab-
> lishment (Mt 9:13 etc). This principle is unfolded
> throughout Jesus' mediatory and priestly work,
> from the incarnation to the crucifixion and glori-
> fication (Ps 39:7–9 equals Heb 10:6–8; cf Phil
> 2:5–11).

In a similar manner Vanhoye stresses the absence
of any ritual, cultic elements in the crucifixion, and
goes on to say: 'Cultic conceptions attain their perfect fulfilment in Christ; that is, they are not taken
over unchanged, but are transformed in an unheard-
of fashion.'[60] Here, surely, we approach the vanish-
ing-point of any real distinction between the literal
and the metaphorical: however, because of the
closely woven texture of Hebrews, so brilliantly demonstrated by Vanhoye, and also the many 'allegorical' and, in the mediaeval sense of the term,
typological, elements we have found in Hebrews, the

[60] A. Romeo, the article-chapter 'La spiritualizzazione del
culto', in *Enciclopedia del sacerdozio*, ed G. Cacciatore, Florence
1953, 504, 507. Vanhoye, in the article 'De Christologia . . .', 57–
58. For students of the history and background of the Second
Vatican Council there is a certain piquancy in quoting Mgr
Romeo and a member of the staff of the *Biblicum* in a single
footnote; I beg the indulgence of both writers.

metaphorical reading seems to me much the more plausible.

The next subdivision, concerned with the new covenant, need not detain us so long. The use of the word *diathēkē*, which may mean either 'will' or 'covenant-alliance' is a famous *crux interpretum*: some hold that the word is deliberately used in both senses in this passage, others that the meaning 'covenant-alliance' is consistent throughout. Fortunately, since both interpretations are in agreement that *diathēkē* in 9 : 15 and 20 mean 'covenant-alliance', and these verses are the important ones for an examination of the typology of Hebrews, we may, here and in the bibliography, neglect the oceans of printers' ink that have been expended upon this question. We may concern ourselves immediately with the typology of the Sinai covenant in relation to the death of Christ.

It is certain that the oldest texts regarding Moses, including especially the composite text in Ex 24 from the Elohistic and Yahwistic sources, do not portray him as a priest nor regard the covenant-making as a priestly ritual. Those interpreters, therefore, who deduce a formally priestly office of Christ from the fact that he is called 'the mediator of a new covenant' might usefully pause and ask themselves how far they are justified either by Ex 24 or by Jer 31 in making such a deduction.[61] Not, of course, that

[61] See Cullmann, *The Christology...*, 100: 'It is because of the

Hebrews offers a scientific, historical and critical exegesis of Exodus or Jeremiah; given the very great difference in the historical situations, his and ours, the author of Hebrews necessarily approaches these texts with a quite different set of principles of interpretation.

On the theory that *diathēkē*, in this passage, is used deliberately in a double sense, we are clearly confronted with a piece of word-play that belongs to the field of metaphor. If, on the other hand, it means 'covenant-alliance' throughout, then the statement that 'where a *diathēkē* is involved, the death of the one who made it must be established' will not fit all the descriptions of covenant-making we actually find in the Old Testament, even granted that the death is a 'sacramental' death in the death of the slain animal of the covenant sacrifice for, as we have already noted, there is no mention of a blood sacrifice at the covenant-making at Shechem, whatever the historical facts of the case. And it was the Shechem covenant that constituted the sacral people 'Israel', the sacred confederation of the twelve tribes.

---

once-for-all character of Jesus' atoning act that the writer of Hebrews emphasises so strongly that as High Priest Jesus mediated a *New Covenant* with God. "Therefore he is the mediator of a new covenant" (Heb 9:15). Heb 12:24 too refers to him as *diathēkēs neas mesitēs*. In this respect the concept of High Priest comes in contact again with that of the *ebed Yahweh*, whose function is *also* the re-establishment of the covenant with God.' (The italics in 'also' are mine.) The motif of the servant in Hebrews will be examined at 9:28.

Further, the mention of the scarlet wool and hyssop in 9:19 does not belong to the account of the Sinai covenant at all, but is imported from Nm 19:6 in order to suggest the theme of sin-offering. If the words 'and goats' are to be read in the phrase 'the blood of calves and goats'[62] it is imported from Lv 16 for the same reason. And the description in Exodus makes no mention of the sprinkling of the book, it speaks instead of the pouring out of half the blood against the altar, which clearly represents God's presence among his people. This is a puzzling change that will be discussed in relation to 9:23; the change seems, in any case, to belong with those 'allegorical' procedures we have so often encountered. Moses' words, as we have seen, have been altered in order to bring them nearer in line with the traditional cup-saying from the last supper. The description of the consecration of the tent and its furniture in Ex 40:9–11 speaks of an anointing with oil, not with blood, in contrast with Heb 9:21. And finally the words 'indeed, under the law almost everything is purified with blood, and without the shedding of blood there is no forgiveness of sins' are apparently intended to look backwards over the whole description of covenant and consecration, which apparently

[62] With Sinaiticus, Alexandrinus, *Ephraemi Rescriptus*, Claromontanus, the Itala manuscripts and the Vulgate. The Aland-Black-Metzger-Wikgren text chooses the other reading, but grants it only third-class certainty. It is easy to see why scribes could have omitted the words.

procured a forgiveness of sins, that is, according to 9:13 'a purification of the flesh'. The second half of the verse also looks forward: without the shedding of the blood of Christ there is no forgiveness of sins so far as conscience is concerned.

The inclusions on 'blood', verses 18 and 22, and upon 'Christ', verses 24 and 28, leave verse 23 in a somewhat indeterminate position; nevertheless the echo of 'necessity' (RSV 'must') from verse 16 and of 'purified' from verse 22 place it firmly, as we have seen, following Vanhoye, with 9:15–22. It is a very puzzling verse; what are we to make of the statement 'the heavenly things themselves (must be purified) with better sacrifices than these'? What are the heavenly things and why do they need to be purified? Vanhoye has argued[63] that the 'heavenly things' of 9:23 are parallel with the book, the people, the tent and the vessels of 9:19, 20. His argument is, however, rather forced. He states roundly: 'We are faced with a dilemma, therefore, between these two: either the dedication is a mere ceremony lacking in any kind of effectiveness, and then the sacrifice of Christ is a gratuitous piece of cruelty, or the sacrificial dedication was necessary, which implies that the heavenly sanctuary was unclean or profane.' Vanhoye is then able to insist upon a distinction between the heavens and the heavenly things, and to

---

[63] 'Mundatio per sanguinem' (Heb 9:22–23), *Verbum Domini* XLIV (1966); the quotation is from p 185.

suggest an identification for these. But it should perhaps first be noted that if the sacrificial and priestly
language of Hebrews is taken as a biblical image
then the dilemma falls away of itself. Even if the
dilemma falls away, however, this does not necessarily mean that the suggested parallels fall away:
the way is still open for an identification of the tent
with 'the mystery of the glorified body of Christ', all
the people with 'the Church of Christ', the book
with 'the word of Christ' and the vessels used in worship with 'the sacraments', and especially baptism
(10:22) and eucharist (13:10). (I am very uncertain
of the correctness of this last reference; I would
accept a reference to 6:4, where with eg Héring I
see a reference to the eucharist.)[64] Vanhoye himself
is somewhat diffident about the last identification,
and his attempt to solve the puzzle of the book of 9:19
is not notably successful: while it is true that it was
only after the death and resurrection of Jesus that
the Spirit led the disciples into the truth of Jesus'
word (Jn 16:13), it seems rather forced to identify
this with the *purification* of the heavenly book. Vanhoye's point that it is the heavenly things, not
heaven, that are said to be purified, is well taken,
and one may admit a general parallel with 9:19–21;
further than that it seems perilous to go.

The last subdivision, 9:24–28, will concern us
particularly in our next chapter, for it is in these

[64] *Ib*, 188–191.

verses that the realised eschatology of Hebrews is most emphatically stated. In 9:24 'a sanctuary made with hands' is contrasted with 'heaven itself', as 'a copy (*antitupos*) of the true one' is contrasted with 'the presence (literally "face") of God'.[65] Yet clearly the 'sanctuary made with hands' is reminiscent, by way of contrast, of 'the greater and more perfect tent, not made with hands, that is, not of this creation' of 9:11, which was identified with the risen body of Christ. Hebrews does not work with a rigid set of typological identifications: the living movement of his thought leads him far in the direction of mixing his metaphors, as the poets also regularly do. In 9:25 'to offer himself (not repeatedly)' is contrasted with 'enters... (yearly) with blood not his own'. We have seen that in 9:7 the high priest is said to offer the blood; I think, therefore, that the idea of Christ offering his blood is latent here, for 'the life of the flesh is in the blood' (Lv 17:11), and in offering his blood Christ offers himself.

The liturgy of the day of atonement clearly dominates this subdivision, as indeed it was not absent even from the last, that was directly and ostensibly concerned with the new covenant. It is with no surprise therefore that we learn that Jesus 'appears in the presence of God on our behalf' (9:24), and has 'appeared (a different but related verb)... to put away sin by the sacrifice of himself'. With 9:28 a

---

[65] Vanhoye, *La structure*..., 154.

new motif appears: 'Christ having been offered . . . to bear the sins of many', where 'many', especially in this context of judgment (9:27) and the bearing of sins, is reminiscent of the fourth servant song of Isaiah, 52:13–53:12, especially of 53:12: 'he bore the sin of many, and made intercession for the transgressors'.[66] There are many sacrificial motifs in this song[67]; whether they may usefully be described as priestly is more doubtful. To present the guilt-offering (*asham*, Lv 5 and 7:1–10) is undoubtedly a priestly function, but since there is an obvious element of transference here, it is not at all clear that we can deduce that the servant is to be regarded as a priest. When we look more closely at the kind of transference involved, caution in this matter seems a matter of inexorable necessity. For, in the first place, it is a question of the self-offering of the servant and, as we have seen, Israel was excluded forever from the offering of human sacrifice. Again, it is by no means certain whether the servant simply *is* Israel or merely represents Israel; in view of the situation of the Babylonian exile and the undoubted identification of Israel with the servant in the chapters surrounding the four servant songs, I am in-

[66] Bruce, *ad loc*: 'The language here is a plain echo of the fourth Servant Song'.

[67] See eg M. Barth, 9, n 1. Barth has a tendency to exaggerate; both 'peace' and 'account' are taken to be sacrificial words, whereas they are words that occur in many contexts, including sacrificial ones, but primarily in military and everyday situations respectively.

clined to adopt the first interpretation as closer to the original, literal meaning. Again, a lesser but still significant element, the servant is compared to 'a lamb that is led to the slaughter', perhaps, as most commentators think, a sacrificial lamb; this introduces an inescapable element of metaphor into the song. I read the fourth servant song as a most moving interpretation, in the symbolic language we find so often in the bible, of the mystery of the Lord's will and design in the fall of the messianic people and their suffering in exile. Hebrews reads Is 52–53 christologically; this gives us no justification for doing the same when it is a question, as it must be the question, of attempting a literal (though of course literary and therefore poetic) interpretation of the text in second Isaiah.

Third Section: source of eternal salvation, 10:1–18

We have seen some evidence above for regarding this section as both completing our picture of Christ as source of salvation and as bringing out the effectiveness of this salvation with regard to those who are saved. In particular, an interpretation of the use of Ps 40:6–8 has already been attempted. There are, nevertheless, still some points to be noted. Verses 1–3 deduce an ineffectiveness of the propitiatory liturgy of the day of atonement from the mere fact of its annual occurrence: it is therefore merely 'a reminder of sin year after year'. We have seen

rabbinical evidence above that this is not the conception of late judaism; nor can it claim to be a literal
exegesis of Lv 16. The ritual of the day of atonement
was repeated yearly in order to make atonement for
the sins of that year precisely, as the rabbinical idea
of 'suspension' makes clear. Even 10:4, 'For it is impossible that the blood of bulls and goats should take
away sins', bears the marks of what Moule has called
'a no-sacrifice apologia'. Clearly, animal sacrifices
could not procure the forgiveness of sins in a mech-
anical or magical fashion, but this is excluded in
Leviticus by the insistence that the ritual is a commandment of the Lord, a gift of the Lord to his
people. The *Mishnah*, which, though written later
than Hebrews, is usually reporting older traditions,
emphasises the need for repentance: the man who
says he will sin and repent later will not be given
the opportunity and for him the day of atonement
will be of no help (Yoma 8:9). Atonement is ultimately God's work rather than man's,[68] and the faithful observance of every detail of the ritual was a sign
of repentance and trust in God.[69]

Verses 11–14 make a final contrast between the
Old Testament priesthood and our high priest: the
first ministered standing, but this one has sat down
at the right hand of God; the first was daily at his
service, this one awaits until his enemies should be

[68] Yoma 6:2. See M. Barth, 21–26.
[69] See, once again, the article from St Thomas, *Summa Theologiae* iiia. 62. 6.

made a stool for his feet (the old royal sign of victory); the first offered the same sacrifices repeatedly, this one offered a single sacrifice; the first sacrifices can never take away sins, this one offered truly for sins, 'for by a single offering he has perfected for all time those who are sanctified'.[70] With Jesus' session at the right hand of God we look right back over the long development upon priesthood to the introduction to the epistle. The long third part is not yet completed however; there is first a short paragraph recalling the text from Jeremiah concerning the new covenant written in the heart and the forgiveness of sins that accompanies it, and drawing the conclusion that 'where there is forgiveness of these, there is no longer any offering for sin'. Upon this there follows the conclusion to the whole third part, 10: 19–39.

From this conclusion, only the first paragraph need concern us here (10: 19–25). The theme of the whole is exhortatory, but here, as always, this has a firm doctrinal basis. The centre of the paragraph, which is one long sentence, consists of three exhortatory 'let us' phrases based upon the three virtues of faith, hope and love. We are first told that 'we have confidence to enter the sanctuary by the blood of Jesus' before being exhorted to 'draw near with a true heart in full assurance of faith'. Clearly, the typology of the day of atonement is here applied to all christians, and this, of course, presupposes Jesus'

[70] Vanhoye, 167.

own entry into the heavenly sanctuary: 'by the new and living way which he opened for us through the curtain, that is, through his flesh' (10:20). Here the 'flesh' of Jesus is identified with the curtain that marked off the holy of holies,[71] as his risen body was identified with the tent not made with hands in 9:11. Since 'flesh' is so often in the bible that which passes away ('all flesh is grass', Is 40:6), there is an evident appropriateness in this imagery. Yet 'flesh' and 'body' are ultimately identical: it is the flesh of Jesus that is raised as spirit (1 Cor 15:45; cf Heb 9:13–14). The cultic overtones of the verb 'to draw near' are particularly evident in this paragraph: 'since we have a great priest over the house of God, let us draw near'.

Fourth part: faith and endurance, 11: 1–12:13

The two themes of the fourth part of the epistle, 11:1–12:13, are announced in 10:39, 'faith', the subject of 11:1–40, and in 10:36, 'endurance', the subject of 12:1–13. The sacrificial typologies of Abraham and Moses in chapter 11 have already been noted. More remarkable, in view of exaggeratedly 'priestly' interpretations of the epistle, is the reference to the cross in 12:2–3, which is quite devoid of any priestly or ritual language: 'looking to Jesus

[71] For the suggestion that 'that is, through his flesh' refers back to 'the way', see eg Héring *comm in loc*.

the pioneer and perfecter of our (RSV; the Greek has no "our", which leaves open the possibility that for Hebrews Jesus is not only "faithful" (3 : 6) but also *the* man of faith[72]) faith, who for the joy[73] that was set before him endured the cross, despising the shame, and is seated at the right hand of the throne of God.[74] Consider him who endured from sinners such hostility against himself, so that you may not grow weary or faint-hearted.' Although there are no overt references to priesthood or ritual here, there are some verbal linkages with other passages of the epistle that have: 'pioneer of faith' is reminiscent of 'pioneer of their salvation' (2 : 10) (and conceptually of 'forerunner', 6 : 20); 'perfecter of faith' is again reminiscent of 2 : 10, since there the pioneer is made 'perfect through suffering', and 'being made perfect' (5 : 9) and 'made perfect for ever' (7 : 28) is the theme, there announced, of the central priesthood

[72] Bruce, *comm in loc*: 'Not only is Jesus the pioneer of faith; in him faith has reached its perfection. . . . The whole life of Jesus was characterised by unbroken and unquestioning faith in his heavenly Father, and never more so than when in Gethsemane He committed Himself to His Father's hands for the ordeal of the cross with the words: "not what I will, but what thou wilt" (Mk 14 : 36).' Bruce, of course, understands 'faith' in its primary New Testament meaning of trust and obedience.

[73] 'For the joy' could mean either 'instead of the joy' or 'in order to gain the joy'. Bruce points out that 'for' (*anti*) is used in 12 : 16 with the meaning 'in order to gain': Esau 'sold his birthright for a single meal'. Vanhoye suggests 'instead of' (*au lieu de*).

[74] Vanhoye points to the parallel between 'perseverance' (*hupomonē*) 12 : 1 and 'endured' (*hupomemenōkota*) 12 : 3, and therefore, rightly, uses only a semi-colon at the end of 12.2.

5*

section of the third part, as we have seen. Finally, 'seated at the right hand of the throne of God' is taken from Ps 110:1, which has so often been quoted in the epistle: 1:3; 8:1; 10:12.

Fifth part: the peaceful fruit of righteousness, 12:14-13:18

The theme of the fifth part is announced at 12:11 and the word 'peace' is repeated in the first verse of the new part, 12:14. We may turn directly to 13:9-16, which is particularly relevant to our theme.[75] The phrase 'strange teachings' of 13:9 is puzzling to commentators, since the rest of the verse and the following ones are concerned once again with the typology and supersession of Old Testament sacrifices; but how can these be called 'strange'? Verse 9b insists once again that the old sacrifices did not benefit their adherents, in contrast to the grace of Christ that truly strengthens hearts. We have seen, with Moule, the parallel between 13:10 'we have an altar' and 8:1 'we have such a high priest'. It is more difficult to identify the altar and to decide what the apparently implied right of christians, in contrast with 'those who serve the (old) tent', to eat from it is meant to signify.[76] A eucharistic interpre-

[75] We have already noted the 'sprinkled blood' of 12:24.

[76] F. V. Filson, in his short book 'Yesterday'. A study of Hebrews in the light of Chapter 13, London 1963, 48-64, suggests that the tent is the heavenly sanctuary and the altar the heavenly altar, and that those who serve the tent are christians. The passage is

tation has often been attempted, especially by catholic commentators,[77] but this seems too close to contradiction of 13 : 9 'it is well that the heart be strengthened by grace, not by foods' for comfort. The eucharist is, of course, grace; but the food symbolism is an essential part of the sacrament. Without supposing that the author of Hebrews belonged to a christian community that did not celebrate the eucharist, or that he is combating a sacrificial interpretation of the eucharist, it is possible to read this verse as one in which 'to eat' means to participate in whatever way in the sacrifice of Christ. For as Spicq remarks very justly, it is only from the time of St Cyprian that the table of the eucharist is called an 'altar'; by Ignatius, Polycarp, Clement of Alexandria and Tertullian it is used symbolically of the sacrifice of Christ.[78] Spicq recommends a similar in-

---

then read as a rejection of 'any idea that Jesus as the once-for-all offering for sin can be thought of as eaten at Christian meals' (p 54). I think Filson is right in rejecting an identification of the altar with the table of the eucharist, but his idea that Hebrews wishes to reject belief in the bodily presence of the Lord in the eucharist is forced and strained, and introduces a formal contradiction of 1 Cor 11 : 27–29, a strange thing in an author so pauline as Hebrews.

[77] Eg J. Swetnam in his article already cited. Spicq is more reserved, but admits an indirect reference to the eucharist; so too Vanhoye in his article 'Mundatio per sanguinem', 190–191. Of course the eucharist is *one* of the ways in which christians 'eat from the altar', ie participate in the sacrifice of Christ, but it cannot be directly in the author's mind here, unless we are to suppose that his argument is hopelessly confused.

[78] Spicq, *comm in loc.*

terpretation here, though he particularises this still further and suggests that we should think of the body of Christ, rather than of the cross. This is an interesting suggestion, since the body of Christ has already been metaphorically identified with the heavenly tent 9:11 and with the veil 10:20.

Verse 11 provides a typological justification for the exclusion of 'those who serve the tent' from participation from the altar, using once again the ritual of the day of atonement: 'For the bodies of those animals whose blood is brought into the sanctuary by the high priest as a sacrifice for sins are burned outside the camp.' Verse 12 then finds an application of this to the history of Jesus: 'So Jesus also suffered outside the gate in order to sanctify the people through his own blood'; and verse 13 an application to christian life: 'Therefore let us go forth to him outside the camp, bearing abuse for him'.[79]

[79] Bruce, commenting on 13:12, suggests that the author has in mind also the slaughtering of the red heifer, which took place outside the camp. The 'camp' of 13:13 may mean either this present sinful world, as 13:15 at first sight seems to suggest: 'here we have no lasting city', or judaism, in keeping with the theme of the whole epistle. Spicq prefers the second view; he quotes for the first a whole series of interpreters from Cyril and Chrysostom to Windisch and Cambier, and for the second Theodoret, Westcott and 'most of the moderns'. Héring follows the first interpretation, while suggesting as a secondary meaning, if the readers are living in Jerusalem, an exhortation to leave the city before the final catastrophe foretold in Mk 13:14. Bruce takes the second view without even discussing the first. Filson has a particularly thorough discussion, pp 60–65, and adds, only to

Then, as we have seen, verses 15–16 exhort the readers to the practice of the christian life in sacrificial terms: 'Through him then let us continually offer up a sacrifice of praise to God, that is, the fruit of lips that acknowledge his name. Do not neglect to do good and to share what you have, for such sacrifices are pleasing to God.' It is evident that such sacrifices are only made possible by the sacrifice of Christ 'outside the gate', and that these sacrifices are acceptable only when offered by those who have been sanctified through his blood (13:12). It is possible that it is here that we should find an implicit reference to the eucharist, rather than in 13:10; 'a sacrifice of praise' (*thusia aineseōs*) is practically identical with 'eucharist' (thanksgiving) in meaning (see Lv 7:2 in the LXX and 7:12, the same verse, in the TM).[80]

We have now completed our study of the 'alle-

---

reject it and adopt instead the second interpretation above, a third possibility, after the pattern of the Qumran community: to withdraw from the city into the wilderness.

[80] The footnote in RSV to 13:15 sends one first to Lv 7:12. Lv 7:12–15 is concerned with the sacrifice of peace offerings for a thanksgiving. The phrase *thusia aineseōs*, sacrifice of praise, is used both in Heb 13:15 and in Lv 7:12 in the LXX translation (where it is numbered 7:2). Spicq refers to a rabbinic tradition that in the time of Messiah all sacrifices will be abolished except for the thanksgiving sacrifice which shall remain for ever. Behm, in his article *thusia* in TWNT III, 186, refers 13:15–16 back to 10:5f, and sees an equivalent meaning for 'sacrifice' in both texts: self-offering, the submission of one's will to the action of God.

gorical' typology of priesthood in Hebrews. At many points we have encountered the realised eschatology of the epistle; our next chapter will consider this theme directly and place it in relation to the theme of priesthood.

4
Image and eschatology in Hebrews

That the imagery of priesthood and sacrifice in Hebrews is a piece of 'allegorical' typology was the burden of chapter 3. But is this imagery and typology fundamentally biblical in character, based upon a linear conception of time and of the working out of God's purpose in time, or is it rather platonic or hellenistic in character, under the influence of Philo and Alexandrian judaism? It is not to our purpose here to discuss exactly how far Philo and Alexandrian judaism were platonic, and how far they were or were not faithful to the jewish and biblical heritage; it will suffice to state briefly the meaning of the platonic conception of time and eternity, and to go on to examine the state of opinion on that basis. This method of procedure does not imply that I share the over-simplified conception of the contrast between Greek and Hebrew thought so severely criticised by J. Barr[1]; but it is plain, on the one hand, that there is no room in Plato's philosophy for a structure of thought and view of the world based ultimately upon the eschatological action of God in history; on the other hand the question must be squarely faced: is there room for such eschatological action in the thought-world of Hebrews?

Plato's conception of the relationship between time and eternity is stated succinctly in a well-known text from the Timaeus:

When the father and creator saw the creature which he had made moving and living, the created image (*agalma*) of the eternal gods, he rejoiced and in his joy determined to make the copy

---

[1] J. Barr, *The semantics of biblical language*, Oxford 1961; also in the second chapter 'Athens or Jerusalem?—The question of distinctiveness' in his *Old and New in Interpretation*, London 1966. Barr admits that there is distinctiveness, though he is in disagreement with many of the ways in which it is stated, and with some of the theological uses to which it is put: 'So long as we are working on the actual ideas, beliefs, philosophies, confessions, stories, and so on, ie on that which is expressed in the actual texts on one side or on the other, there is no reason to doubt that very great differences will usually be found between Hebrew and Greek thought. On the other hand, there is no reason to doubt that certain similarities will appear from time to time. Nevertheless, if we take such notable datum-points as Plato's philosophy as actually expressed and the message of Amos as actually expressed, I do not see any reason to doubt that the contrast is extremely great', *Old and New ...*, 46–47. To Amos the names of Matthew, Mark, Luke and Paul may be added (to take admitted and basic examples of New Testament eschatological theologies), and the question then asked: to which side does Hebrews belong?

still more like the original; and as this was eternal, he sought to make the universe eternal, so far as it might be. Now the nature of the ideal being was everlasting, but to bestow this attribute in its fullness upon a creature was impossible. Wherefore he resolved to make a moving image (*eikō*) of eternity (*aiōn*), and when he set in order the heaven, he made this image eternal but moving according to number, while eternity itself rests in unity; and this image we call time.[2]

Time, for the astronomically-minded Greeks, is not primarily a human affair nor God's voluntary direction and intervention in human affairs, it is a matter of the circular movement of the heavens in which number imitates, defectively, unity, and the moving circle imitates the stillness of the eternal point. The cyclic conception of time was applied to human affairs also, the rise and fall of human societies and the, perhaps with Plato slightly playful, theory that all events endlessly repeat themselves after the great cataclysms that bring each age to a close: once again Socrates will gather his pupils around him in future ages, and so on *ad infinitum*.

What time is to eternity all earthly things are to the eternal heavenly ideas in the philosophy of Plato. The earthly world is one of shadows and images, whatever reality they possess comes from

[2] Timaeus 37, d–e.

their imitation of the eternal forms, the world of the divine ideas. Every earthly shadow-reality has its true eternal perfect counterpart in which it participates. Hebrews uses much the same kind of language to describe the relationship between the old tent and its liturgy and the heavenly tent in which Christ is the liturgical minister (*leitourgos* 8 : 2). But does this imply a platonic structure of thought? And if it does, is such a thought structure the fundamental one in Hebrews, excluding, as it must, any eschatological pattern of thought except of a secondary and superficial kind? Or are we to take the view that the thought of Hebrews is essentially incoherent, that the author is trying to hold together fundamentally incompatible notions?

J. Moffatt inclined to the last solution, not so much in so far as the realised eschatology of Hebrews is concerned, since he did not regard that eschatologically, but in relation to the eschatology still to be realised: the return of Christ. Consider this passage from his introduction:

The presence of God is now attainable as it could not be under the outward cultus of the *skēnē* in the Old Testament, for the complete sacrifice has been offered 'in the realm of the spirit', thus providing for the direct access of the people to their God. The full bliss of the fellowship is still in the future, indeed, it is not to be realised finally until

Jesus returns for his people, for he is as yet only their *prodromos* (6:20). The primitive eschatology required and received this admission from the writer, though it is hardly consonant with his deeper thought. And this is why he quotes for example the old words about Jesus waiting in heaven till his foes are crushed (10:12–13). He is still near enough to the primitive period to share the forward look (see, eg, 2:2f; 9:28; 10:37), and unlike Philo, he does not allow his religious idealism to evaporate his eschatology. But while this note of expectation is sounded now and then, it is held that christians already experience the powers of the world to come. The new and final order has dawned ever since the sacrifice of Jesus was made, and the position of believers is guaranteed.[3]

The significant words of judgment and evaluation in that passage, indicative of Moffatt's final interpretation, are these: 'The primitive eschatology required and received this admission from the writer, though it is hardly consonant with his deeper thought.' It is paradoxical that Moffatt's description of the 'admission' of Hebrews—and is it indeed admission, or rather a statement of his own deepest conceptions and beliefs—amounts to a classic summation of the

[3] J. Moffatt, *The Epistle to the Hebrews*, Edinburgh 1924, intro, 34.

eschatological tension between the 'now' and the 'not yet', between the eschatological event and gifts already realised and those yet to be realised, which much contemporary exegetical opinion, rightly to my mind, regards as fundamental in New Testament theology. If one gives full weight to Moffatt's phrase 'in the realm of the spirit', which is presumably a paraphrase of Heb 9:14's phrase 'through the eternal Spirit', and if one acknowledges that the gift of the Holy Spirit is at least connoted there (I have argued above that the reference is directly to the Spirit of God, in view of 9:8, and that the 'spirit', the person of Jesus in relationship to God, is the connoted meaning), and if one remembers that the gift of the Spirit is precisely an event distinctive of the last times, Jl 2:28–29, quoted in Ac 2:17–18 as proof that the last times have come, then it becomes quite impossible to allow the actuality of realisation to evaporate the eschatology. 'It is held that christians already experience the powers of the world to come'; precisely, and if one takes seriously the fact that they belong to the 'age to come' (RSV, Greek: *dunameis te mellontos aiōnos*), that we possess them only by way of anticipation and pledge, and that they are irrevocably *future* in relation to the church as a whole and individual members of it so far as full possession is concerned, the fact that the 'new and final order has dawned' will be taken for what it is, a dawning, and full respect given to the eschatological tension.

Moffatt's exegetical reason for his judgment appears, I think, a few pages later, where he says:

> When the author writes that Christ 'in the spirit of the eternal' (9:14) offered himself as an unblemished sacrifice to God, he has in mind the contrast between the annual sacrifice on the day of atonement and the sacrifice of Christ which never needed to be repeated, because it had been offered in the spirit and—as we might say—in the eternal order of things. It was a sacrifice bound up with his death in history, but it belonged essentially to the higher order of absolute reality. The writer breathed the Philonic atmosphere in which the eternal Now overshadowed the things of space and time. . . .[4]

---

[4] *Ib*, intro, 43. Moffatt goes on: 'he knew this sacrifice had taken place on the cross, and his problem was one that never confronted Philo, the problem we moderns have to face in the question: How can a single historical fact possess a timeless significance?' With this we may compare his comment on 9:14: 'Christ was both priest and victim; as Son of God he was eternal and spiritual, unlike mortal high-priests (7:16), and, on the other side, unlike a mortal victim. The implication (which underlies all the epistle) is that even in his earthly life Jesus possessed eternal life. Hence what took place in time on the cross, the writer means, took place really in the eternal, absolute order. Christ sacrificed himself *ephapax*, and the single sacrifice needed no repetition, since it possessed eternal absolute value as the action of One who belonged to the eternal absolute order. He died—he had to die—but only once (9:15–10:18) for his sacrifice, by its eternal significance, accomplished at a stroke what no

Moffatt's use of the phrase 'the eternal Now' (we may leave it to philonic scholars to say whether it gives a complete account of Philo's thought or not) is particularly striking: it is not only an attempt to give an account of Hebrews' debt to Philo, but beyond that, and much more, to answer 'the problem we moderns have to face in the question: How can a single historical fact possess a timeless significance?' Moffatt thinks that this can only be done by giving a kind of platonic eternal value, a quality of the really real, to the event upon the cross, and this, he thinks, is precisely what Hebrews does. I have argued, in the second chapter, that Hebrews thinks of the event of the cross as at once earthly and heavenly; this does *not* mean that I share Moffatt's view that the bloody happening upon the cross is somehow a platonic eternal reality at the same time. Hebrews' conception of the heavenly reality of the offering of Christ's blood is, as I have tried to establish earlier, through and through a biblical image: implicit in the imagery, however, is the idea that an event that typologically corresponds to the annual liturgy of the day of atonement has happened 'once for all' in heaven. That Hebrews' conception of

---

amount of animal sacrifices could have secured, viz the forgiveness of sins.' This is accurately and finely stated; it remains only to note that an eternal, absolute order in which a death can *take place* and accomplish *at a stroke* the forgiveness of sins is no longer the eternal, absolute order of Plato's world of the divine ideas.

heaven and of the eternal is a timeless platonic one I take leave to doubt: it does not seem at all to correspond to what Hebrews actually says. That there are philonic, and therefore in some sense hellenistic, and perhaps, given the syncretism of Alexandria, in some remoter sense platonic, words and phrases and even clusters of words and phrases (Spicq calls these, inaccurately to my mind 'patterns of thought', *schèmes de pensée*) in Hebrews is undoubted; it does not seem, however, that Hebrews' conception of heaven and eternity is at all a platonic one. The only eternity that Hebrews knows is that of the living God, who has indeed 'rested on the seventh day from all his works' (4:4), but has by no means been inactive since then, for 'in many and various ways God spoke of old to our fathers by the prophets; but in these last days he has spoken to us by a Son, whom he appointed the heir of all things' (1:1–2) and 'it was fitting that he, for whom and by whom all things exist, in bringing many sons to glory, should make the pioneer of their salvation perfect through suffering' (2:10). And just as God is spending a most active eternity that is closely concerned with the things of earth, so too the 'heaven' of Hebrews that is God's dwelling place is not at all a place where nothing happens: Christ has entered once for all into the Holy Place (9:12), into heaven itself, now to appear in the presence of God on our behalf (9:24). This is of course the language of imagery, but since Hebrews' only account of eternity and of heaven is given in the language of symbolism, it does not seem that Moffatt is right in his platonising interpretation of the epistle.

Moffatt is not alone in this interpretation of the epistle; a fundamentally platonising interpretation is urged by J. Cambier, Spicq, Héring and J. Coppens.[5] There are variations of presentation from

[5] J. Cambier, in his article 'Eschatologie ou Hellénisme dans l'Epître aux Hébreux', *Salesianum* (1949), 62–96, declares that he wishes to take a middle position between a purist jewish reading and an excessively platonising interpretation. But when he reports that he has found formulations (only?) taken from jewish eschatology but an Alexandrian *influence* on the way of thinking (p 63), we may rightly anticipate that the Alexandrian, hellenistic aspect is going to receive pride of place. Cambier's study concentrates upon the final exhortation, which he thinks extends from 13:9 to 13:15 (Vanhoye, rightly, points to the inclusions on 'leaders' in 7 and 17, and 'behaviour' (RSV 'life', Greek *anastrophē*) in 13:7 and 'to behave' (RSV 'act', Greek *anastrephomai*) in 13:18, and so establishes the paragraph 13:7–18) and focuses more particularly still upon 13:14: 'Here we have no lasting city, but we seek the city which is to come.' Cambier's method is to establish a hellenistic use of the verb 'to last' (*menein*) to mean a share in divine eternal reality conceived of after the manner of Plato, and then to trace all uses of the verb 'to come' (*mellein*) through the epistle, suggesting for each one that 'to come' does not really point to the future but to the heavenly. This sentence on 9:11 will indicate the method: 'The word *mellonta*, like the whole of v 11 in which it is found, insists not so much upon the temporal aspect: the good things which are in the future; but rather upon this fact: the good things which Christ wins for us belong to another world.' This interpretation destroys the eschatological tension, it fails to see that the good things to come may only be shared in the present by way of eschatological anticipation until Christ appears a second time to save those who are eagerly waiting for him (9:28).

This authentically evangelical note of eager expectation has disappeared in Cambier's presentation, and that which is 'to come' has disappeared into that which is 'up there'. But in Hebrews the heavenly sanctuary, house, city and homeland, while certainly pictured as being 'up there', are nevertheless truly future in relation to us, though paradoxically we have 'come to Mount Zion and to the city of the living God, the heavenly Jerusalem' (12:22). Paul, in Gal 4:26, and Revelation 21–22, manage to speak of the heavenly Jerusalem without thereby becoming platonists; the same may be said of the author of Hebrews. And the weight placed on the word *menein* in Cambier's argument does not at all succeed in showing that this is a specifically Greek or platonic idea; it is a constant theme of Old Testament thought that God abides, remains; 'Thou, Lord, didst found the earth in the beginning, and the heavens are the work of thy hands; they will perish, but thou remainest' (*diameneis*) (Heb 1:10–11, quoting Ps 102:25–26). We shall see later that the psalmists' theme of the unshakeable city of Zion, eg Ps 46:5, and of course the unshakeable remains, was read in an eschatological, messianic and 'heavenly' way by Hebrews: see 12:26–28 and Vanhoye's commentary upon it in his article 'L'*oikoumenē* dans l'epître aux Hébreux', *Biblica* XLV (1964), 248–253.

Spicq's position is fairly predictable, since, as we have seen, he regards the author of Hebrews as a disciple of Philo. A short quotation will suffice to establish propriety of placing him with Cambier: 'In this epistle the scale of values is not so much that of the present and the future, as in Jewish and the Synoptic apocalyptic, but rather that of the visible and the invisible; more exactly, the visible is reserved for the future, but the substance of reality, even though invisible, is already present: faith gives access to the spiritual world, lets us go behind the veil, into the city of God' (I, 268, n 6). Spicq is more balanced than Cambier, but there can be little doubt that the contrast with the synoptics is too strong, and that the statement above about the rôle of faith slackens the eschatological tension of Heb 11:1: 'Now faith is the assurance of things *hoped for*', and what is hoped for is not yet fully possessed.

Héring, again, belongs with this group, although he excludes a 'thoroughgoing Platonism' (*Platonisme conséquent*) from

Hebrews, p 10. Take, for example, this statement: 'Like Philo, our author accepts a kind of philosophical and cosmological framework which is much more Platonic than biblical. The succession of the two world-ages (the present world-age and the future one), a classic conception in Judaism and primitive christianity, is replaced by two co-existent levels, one on top of the other: the supra-sensible and the phenomenal worlds. The first contains the eternal ideas which the second attempts to reproduce in the material world. The first is "Heaven" for Philo, as also for this epistle', p 10. Once again, the idea of a celestial sanctuary, and for that matter city, is a constant feature of ancient Near Eastern thought, and does not in the least point to a platonic world of eternal ideas. Nor does the commencement of Héring's next paragraph suffice to restore a true balance: 'Nevertheless, the christian sensibility of our author reacts energetically against this Platonising tendency whenever christian hope is at stake.' It is not only the sensibility but also the fundamental intellectual conceptions of Hebrews that are biblical and eschatological, though evangelical realised eschatology (Lk 17:21: 'the kingdom of God is in the midst of you'—probably an authentic saying of Jesus) is necessarily different from jewish unrealised eschatology. It is in no way the less eschatological for that, for it is 'in the last days' (Ac 2:17), that we live.

Finally, Coppens is content to follow Cambier in denying the eschatology of Hebrews any real eschatological force: 'in the Epistle to the Hebrews eschatology undergoes a notable transformation. It is still, no doubt, in some texts, placed in a pattern of chronological development that one might call linear (1:2; 9:26; 10:25, 37; 12:26–27). But this classical and traditional point of view appears somehow in the margin of another extra-temporal conception which seems to be the central idea. The antithesis is no longer so much between present and future as between earthly, passing, transitory realities and heavenly, abiding, eternal ones. In Heb 13:14 there is a reinterpretation of the jewish eschatological city in terms of Alexandrian speculation. The words *mellōn* and *menōn* particularly present us with concepts that treat eschatological realities after the pattern of Alexandrian thinking.' The only argument that is provided is the interpretation of *mellōn* and *menōn*, taken from Cambier; we have already seen just how fragile this argument is.

author to author. Cambier, for example, bases his interpretation on the heavenly, lasting city of 13 : 14, Spicq upon his theory that the author of Hebrews is a disciple of Philo; but the basic idea is already fully present in Moffatt, and Moffatt has the advantage of presenting what he considers merely the lingering remnants of the 'primitive eschatology' with greater objectivity than Cambier.

We may therefore turn to an author who has attempted a really mediating position, A. Cody. He tries to give full acceptance to a jewish, linear conception of time and what he considers an Alexandrian type of eschatological thinking:

> To conclude, then, we can note the orientations of the author's thought. His notion of time is the linear notion of Jewish thought. His notion of eternity has some affinity with that of traditional Judaism—the concept of eternity marking God's point of view, remaining in touch with the rhythmic flow of early history—but his concept of the relation between time and eternity has been radically transformed by the Greek dualism inherited, probably, through the Alexandrian quarter of Judaism. His eschatology is more Alexandrian than Palestinian in its concern more with eternal life than with the resurrection of the body, and it differs from the early eschatology of the Old Testament in its admission of eschatological

events already realised, a point it has in common with the eschatology of Philo, of the Judean sectaries, and especially of the New Testament in general, where all eschatology is referred to Christ. He shares particularly with St John the idea of eternal, celestial realities made actual in time, but retains more of the eschatology of the future and of the *parousia* than does St John.[6]

This is getting much closer to Hebrews in its recognition that realised eschatology and a linear concept of time go together in Hebrews, as in the New Testament generally, and that these are central, not marginal, conceptions in Hebrews. I do not wish to urge a 'purist'[7] jewish reading of Hebrews, as if there would be some special virtue in sustaining a purely biblical conception of God's eternity over against hellenistic notions, but is not Cody's statement that 'his concept of the relation between time and eternity has been radically transformed by the Greek dualism' grossly overstated? That there is a contrast, and a radical one, is presupposed everywhere in the Old Testament, for example in the psalm quoted in the first chapter of Hebrews: 'Thou, Lord, didst found the earth in the beginning, and the heavens are the work of thy hands; they will perish, but thou

---

[6] A. Cody, *Heavenly sanctuary and liturgy in the Epistle to Hebrews*, St Meinrad, Indiana 1960, 143.

[7] J. Barr, *Old and New in interpretation*, 40 and 171–200.

remainest; they will all grow old like a garment, like a mantle thou wilt roll them up, and they will be changed. But thou art the same, and thy years will never end' (1:10–12, quoting Ps 102:25–27; see also the contrast in 1:11–12 and 24 between the days of the psalmist and the years of God that endure for ever). And it may well be that Hebrews shares in the linear notion of eternity as unending 'time' that O. Cullmann has shown to be the normal biblical one, for in 10:12 we read 'But when this one (RSV footnote; the text inserts "Christ") had offered for all time a single sacrifice for sins, he sat down at the right hand of God, then to wait until his enemies should be made a stool for his feet'. The language is symbolic there, and so it is not possible to be certain that the glorified Christ literally 'waits' in heaven; it is clear however that the image is thoroughly unplatonic.

The assertion that the eschatology of Hebrews is 'more Alexandrian than Palestinian in its concern more with eternal life than with the resurrection of the body' might lead us to expect that the phrase 'eternal life' would occur frequently in the epistle. In fact 'life' occurs only twice in our epistle, at 7:3 of Melchizedek who 'has neither beginning of days nor end of life', and at 7:16 of Christ 'who has become a priest, not according to a legal requirement concerning bodily descent but by the power of an indestructible life'. The uses of 'eternal' and 'for eternity' we must examine later; it may be noted at this time that most of them are concerned with the eternal priesthood of Christ (5:6, the proof-text from Ps 110:4 so often repeated) and with the eternal effects of that priesthood (5:9, salvation; 9:12, redemption). The general resurrection is spoken of in 6:2 in a passage that explicitly states that this is one of 'the elementary (and therefore, surely, basic) doctrines of Christ', whether this is thought to form part of the christian catechesis proper, or part of a pre-catechesis presenting doctrines common to judaism and christianity, as some have thought.[8] If Hebrews does not speak more fully of the general resurrection it is because his theme, 'solid food for the mature (with the suggestion of perfection: *teleioi*)' (5:14), is that of the priestly work of Christ. The resurrection of Christ is spoken of only once, but then in the conclusion, which is an emphatic place to put it: 'Now may the God of peace who brought again from the dead our Lord Jesus, the great shepherd of the sheep, by the blood of the eternal covenant . . .', thus associating the resurrection

[8] See eg Bruce, *comm in loc*, who quotes from A. Nairne, *The Epistle of priesthood*, Edinburgh 1913, 15: 'It is significant that the points taken as representing the foundation of penitence and faith are all consistent with Judaism. "Doctrines of washings"— how unnatural are the attempts to explain this plural as referring to Christian Baptism; "imposition of hands, resurrection of dead, eternal judgment"—all this belonged to the creed of a Pharisaic Jew who accepted the whole of the Old Testament.' Bruce adds that it belonged equally to the creed of the Essenes.

with the priestly work of Christ.[9] If the resurrection of Jesus is not spoken of more explicitly in the body of the epistle this is surely because of the structure of the symbolism of the epistle: there is no room for resurrection in the middle of the unfolding ritual of the day of atonement. This is indeed a weakness in the particular typological imagery of the priesthood of Christ in Hebrews, built in, as it is, to the basic structure of the epistle: it does not in the least imply that the resurrection of our Lord Jesus is not of much importance in the mind of the author.

An interpretation of Hebrews along a fundamentally eschatological, realised and to be realised, line seems to be gaining ground of recent years. Not that this is in any way a totally new understanding. Westcott, for example, had already stressed that the eschatological idea of the contrast between 'this age' and 'the age to come' is fundamental in Hebrews.[10] This

[9] Vanhoye, 218, refers the phrase 'who brought again from the dead the great shepherd of the sheep' to Is 63:11, and states, in his footnote 2, 'But it should be noted that if the formulation is new, there is nothing fundamentally heterogeneous: the idea of bringing back up (*remonter*, Greek *anagagōn*) takes up the essential subject of the Epistle, the heavenly fulfilment of the sacrifice of Christ.'

[10] B. F. Westcott, *The Epistle to the Hebrews*, 2nd edn, London 1892, 486: 'But it is on the special revelation of God through Israel and the Christ that the writer of the Epistle chiefly dwells. This falls into two great divisions, corresponding essentially with the two "ages" which sum up for us the divine history of the world, "this age" ("these days") and "the age to come" (6:5). God spake *"in the prophets"* and then *"at the end of these days"*, at the close of the first age, He spake in him who is Son.' To

way of understanding Hebrews is found also in Bonsirven, and has been established by arguments that seem to me irrefutable by C. K. Barrett, F. F. Bruce, and most recently by F. V. Filson.[11] A short examination of the main arguments of these last three will suffice here for our purposes.

C. K. Barrett's essay is a very careful examination

Westcott's remarks it may be added that 'the end of these days' is the time of the once for all sacrifice of Christ (9:26), the time of the new covenant (9:15), in which it is possible to taste the powers of the age to come, 6:5.

[11] J. Bonsirven, *Epître aux Hébreux*, Paris 1943. In his introduction, on p 33, Bonsirven says: 'An extraordinary eschatological conception, which, at one and the same time, holds the present to be future and still awaits another future. The antinomy can only be resolved by a full understanding of the messianic time. In relation to the age of preparation, the evil age, the age of pre-arrangements, shadows and figures, the "present age", Christianity is the age to come. But being set in the material world, unfolding through struggle and temptations, it moves towards the moment of unmixed blessedness. The believer, seeing the fulfilment of prophecy in Christ and the christian dispensation, is convinced that he lives at the time of the maturing of the ages, "at the end of the ages" (9:26), that he is already in "the world to come" (2:5; 6:5), that the good things he enjoys are "the good things to come" (9:11; 10:1). But he knows, all the same, that his homeland is not here below (13:4; 11:10, 14), that the present period of time must have an end at the day of judgment which opens the era of infinite happiness (3:6; 9:28; 10:25; 11:39, 40; 12:14).' C. K. Barrett, 'The eschatology of the Epistle to the Hebrews', in *The background of the New Testament and its eschatology*, already cited, 363–393. F. F. Bruce in his *The Epistle to the Hebrews* and also in his article ' "To the Hebrews" or "To the Essenes" ', in *New Testament Studies* IX (1963), 217–232. F. V. Filson, *'Yesterday'. A study of Hebrews in the light of chapter 13*, London 1967.

of all the eschatological aspects of Hebrews, with perhaps a special emphasis upon unrealised eschatology, but with full recognition of the eschatological character of realised eschatology: 'The covenant inaugurated by Jesus' sacrifice of himself is the fulfilment of prophecy: that is to say, it is an eschatological covenant. Like the Sabbath rest, and the pilgrimage of faith to the city of God, it falls within the scope of the unique Christian eschatology, partly fulfilled and partly forward-looking.'[12] And, one page later: 'He entered (*etsēlthen*), now (*nun*) to appear before God; he has been manifested "now, once, at the consummation of the ages" (*nuni de hapax epi sunteleia tōn aiōnōn*). This "once" refers to an eschatological event that has taken place, and is followed by the plainest assertion of an eschatological event yet to come—the return of Christ (*ophthēsetai tois auton apekdechomenois*).' And Barrett's whole examination of Hebrews leads into this conclusion: 'This review of the sacrifice offered in the heavenly tabernacle by Christ as high priest, bears out, beyond reasonable doubt, the view that the framework of thought in Hebrews is eschatological.' I have no possible modification to propose to any of that.[13]

In his article ' "To the Hebrews" or "to the

---

[12] C. K. Barrett, 384.
[13] *Ib*, 386. Barrett is well aware of the eternal being of the heavenly sanctuary: 'The heavenly tabernacle and its ministrations are from one point of view eternal archetypes, from another, they are eschatological events.'

Essenes" ' F. F. Bruce took up the question of a platonic influence upon the writer of Hebrews through Philo:

> The Epistle certainly manifests impressive affinities with Philo in style and vocabulary; the evidence presented by Père Spicq is adequate on this score. But its very affinities with Philo in style and vocabulary throw into relief the absence of Philonic thought-forms from our author's basic argument. His portrayal of the earthly sanctuary as a copy of the 'real' one in heaven is strongly reminiscent of Platonism; but, when we come to look at it more closely, it is evident that he draws primarily on the instruction to Moses in Ex 25 : 40 'See that you make everything according to the model you saw on the mount'—and he develops this idea in much the same way as apocalyptic writers do, including the New Testament Apocalyptist, who has not generally been regarded as influenced by Plato.[14]

To this argument from the parallel with jewish apocalyptic Bruce adds, in his commentary, an interesting and useful comment upon the idea of the 'shadow' in Hebrews, showing how this conception too is eschatological: 'There is indeed some affinity with platonic idealism here (he is commenting on 8 : 5), but it is our author's language, and not his

[14] *Art cit*, 229–230.

essential thought, that exhibits such affinity. For him, the relation between the two sanctuaries is basically a temporal one. If the earthly sanctuary is a "shadow" of the heavenly, it is because the whole Levitical order *foreshadowed* the spiritual order of the new age.'[15] In his footnote Bruce makes a comparison with the well-known image in Col 2 : 17: 'Therefore let no one pass judgment on you in questions of food and drink or with regard to a festival or a new moon or a sabbath. These are only a shadow of what is to come; but the substance (so RSV; the Greek has "body", *sōma*) belongs to Christ.' It is generally believed that there are hellenistic influences at work upon Colossians, but this passage is purely jewish in its concern, or rather unconcern, about jewish food taboos and festivals, and in its contrast of the shadow with the body. The 'body' is perhaps not merely the substantive reality in contrast with the transitory anticipations of Old Testament times, but is the heavenly resurrected body of him who is the head of the body which is the church. The whole context in Colossians is concerned with the crucified and resurrected body of Christ and with his greater body which is the church. In Hebrews, too, the heavenly reality, the greater and more perfect tent not made with hands (9 : 11) is to

[15] Bruce, *The Epistle to the Hebrews*, 166. The more detailed examination of the context in Colossians and the parallels in Heb 9 : 11 and 3 : 6 is my own.

be identified with the body of Christ, as we have
seen, and the house of God over which Christ is
faithful as a son (3 : 6) is the community of believers.
The parallel between Hebrews and Colossians is
therefore a very close one.

F. V. Filson's book '*Yesterday*' rests upon the idea
that the basic structure of thought in Hebrews is
eschatological rather than spatial, and that this structure is especially evident in the word 'yesterday' of
13 : 8, which has so often, and wrongly, been read in
a timeless platonising fashion:

> This puts before us a basic question. What for the
> writer of Hebrews was the nature of ultimate
> reality? Was it time with its sequence of historical
> events as the key to a sound understanding of life?
> Or was it space as a symbol of two realms of life,
> one of which—and that a secondary one—was this
> earthly time-bound order, while the other—and
> that the truly significant one—was the transcen-
> dent order? In the centuries of New Testament
> interpretation there has been a persistent tendency
> to regard the writer of Hebrews as essentially
> Platonic in his outlook and thought. To him, it
> is often supposed, time with its sequence of events
> is not the proper or adequate form in which to
> state the essential Christian gospel.
>
> But 13 : 8 does not embody a basically Platonic
> point of view. The key word that points away

from an essentially Platonic, basically timeless manner of thought is 'yesterday'. To be sure, if as has been suggested we were to take this word to refer to all previous time and so to mean 'from all eternity', the ideas of time and change would not be dominant. But 'yesterday' does not mean 'from all eternity' or 'throughout the vast vistas of preceding time'. It points to Jesus Christ as one who has just recently become what he now is and what he always will be in all the endless succession of future ages.[16]

There is a slight whiff of the 'purist', in James Barr's sense, about Filson's way of speaking, but I think that his two basic points, that the thought-structure of Hebrews is fundamentally eschatological and that this emerges particularly in the word 'yesterday' which contains in itself in a particularly vivid manner the theme of realised eschatology, are well made. It is one of the curiosities of history that Hebrews, which emerged at the reformation as the biblical bulwark against any mistaken theory of a repetition of the sacrifice of Calvary in the mass (and Trent's decree upon the eucharist is squarely based upon the once for all realised eschatology of Hebrews) should also have been interpreted as a basically platonic work. Vanhoye's study of the literary form of Hebrews has disclosed a three-fold pattern that, to

[16] F. V. Filson, 'Yesterday', 32.

some extent, cuts across the formal division of the parts: this pattern is one of eschatology, ecclesiology and sacrifice. And these three themes are finally to be seen in terms of the contrast between 'the present eon' and the 'eon to come'.[17] This contrast can best be seen in an examination of the apparently opposed time and eternity words in Hebrews, on the one hand 'once' and 'once for all' (*hapax* and *ephapax*), and on the other 'eternity' and 'eternal' (*aiōn* and *aiōnios*); let us now turn to an examination of these.

The adjective 'eternal' occurs six times in Hebrews, and only once is a timeless significance possible even at first sight. That is in the passage at 9:14 where it is said of Christ that it was through the eternal Spirit that he offered himself. We have already discussed the meaning of 'Spirit' in this passage, and found in the proximity of 'the Holy Spirit' in 9:8 reason for thinking of the Holy Spirit in 9:14 also. But we saw also that the spirit which Christ has, or better is, was necessarily connoted in this passage. The parallel with 7:16, 'who has become a priest ... by the power of an indestructible life', though it does not necessarily, to my mind, indicate the reading 'spirit' at 9:14, does of course throw light on that passage: the eternal Spirit of God communicates his eternity (as also his spirituality) to the human spirit of Jesus in the moment when Jesus is perfected, through suffering (2.10), and becomes

[17] Vanhoye, 238–252.

the source of eternal salvation to all who obey him
(5:9), a Son who has been made perfect for ever
(7:28). No doubt the eternal divine nature of Christ
is not absent from the mind of the author at 9:14,
but it is latent rather than manifest there, on this
interpretation. And it is clear that the word 'eternal',
on this theory, is used in a biblical rather than a
platonic manner, and is to be interpreted against a
background of thought that contrasts the power of
God's Spirit with the fragility of flesh (Is 31:1–3)
and the pauline idea that the risen Christ is spirit,
not flesh (1 Cor 15:45).

The other uses of the word 'eternal' in Hebrews
are all concerned with the enduring power of the
saving event of Christ's death, with the exception of
6:2 which speaks of the eternal judgment, clearly
an eschatological, not a platonically timeless, idea.
The other passages speak of eternal salvation (5:9),
eternal redemption (9:12), the promised eternal in-
heritance (9:15) and finally of the eternal covenant
(13:20). There is nothing remotely platonic in any
of these passages.

The word 'eternity', 'eon', occurs most frequently
(six times out of thirteen) in the quotations of Ps
110:4: 'Thou art a priest for ever (*eis ton aiōna*),
after the order of Melchizedek', at 5:6; 6:20; 7:17;
7:21; 7:24 (in the form 'he holds his priesthood
permanently, because he continues for ever') and in
7:28: 'the law appoints men in their weakness as

high priests, but the word of the oath, which came later than the law, appoints a Son (ie as priest) who has been made perfect for ever'. The great saying of 13 : 8: 'Jesus Christ is the same yesterday and to-day and for ever' is closely related to these passages, for, as Filson has shown, 'yesterday' refers to the saving event upon the cross, a work that Hebrews consistently presents in the typological language of priesthood. The priesthood of Jesus is a royal priesthood, and so we find Ps 45 : 6 applied to him in 1 : 8: 'Thy throne, O God, is for ever and ever'. We have seen that the word 'glory' (*doxa*) has priestly associations in Hebrews, so that the motif of priesthood colours even the final doxology of Hebrews: 'that you may do his will, working in you that which is pleasing in his sight, through Jesus Christ; to whom be glory for ever and ever. Amen' (13 : 21).[18]

There are, however, two apparently cosmological uses of the word in which it seems to be equivalent to 'world' (*kosmos* 10 : 5): 'in these last days he has spoken to us by a Son, whom he appointed heir of all things, through whom also he created the world (Greek: *tous aiōnas*) (1 : 2), and 'By faith we understand that the world (Greek: *tous aiōnas*) was created

---

[18] It is not certain whether the final doxology is addressed to the Father or the Son. Vanhoye remarks that the structure of this passage is rather ambivalent, and suggests that this may be deliberate, that the doxology refers both to the Father and to the Son, as Aimo of Auxerre thought: 'cui est gloria, id est Deo Patri et Jesu Christo.' Vanhoye, 217–218 and n 1.

by the word of God, so that what is seen was made out of things which do not appear' (11 : 3). The second of these two texts is at first sight clearly spatial in character, even platonic, as Héring thinks: 'Before going on to list the heroes of old our epistle states a most interesting theological thesis: if we did not have faith we might believe that the visible world is eternal, and that the phenomenal world (another platonic expression!) is in some way self-explanatory. This is exactly Saint Thomas Aquinas' position, who chooses the doctrine that the created world is not eternal because this is the teaching of revelation, that is to say of faith, as our author puts it.'[19] One is reminded of T. Boman's thesis that the Greek way of thinking of the world depends upon a primary apprehension in a visual mode, which gives rise to a static spatial image, while the Hebrew depends upon a kinetic apprehension through movement, which gives rise to a dynamic and time-stamped picture.[20] But if one looks more closely at 11 : 3 the case for a platonic thought structure underlying this verse does not seem proven. It is true that the use of the participle *phainomena* to indicate visible things in general is hellenistic rather than biblical. But the verse is clearly reminiscent

---

[19] Héring, *comm in loc.*
[20] T. Boman, *Hebrew thought compared with Greek*, London 1960.

6*

of the first creation story in Genesis, as also of Ps
33 : 6: 'By the word of the Lord the heavens were
made, and all their host by the breath of his mouth'
and 8–9 'Let all the earth fear the Lord, let all the
inhabitants of the world stand in awe of him! For
he spoke, and it came to be; he commanded, and it
stood forth'. One can compare also Ps 89 : 37–38 for
the use of the word 'make', 'fashion': 'His seed en-
dures for ever, and his throne like the sun before
me, and like the moon that has been fashioned
for ever (*katērtismenē eis ton aiōna*). And the faithful
witness in the heaven.' (I have given a literal translation of the Greek.) Heb 11 : 3 begins 'By faith we
understand that the world was created (*katērttsthai*)'.
Vanhoye has pointed out the inclusion on the words
'things not seen' and 'events as yet unseen' in 11 : 1
and 7, as also the repetition of 'seen' in the phrase
'what is seen' in verse 3, with the remark that
these are the only uses of the word (*blepomenon*) in
Hebrews.[21] The 'things not seen' of 11 : 1 are identical with 'the things hoped for'; with these the
visible world is contrasted in 11 : 3. The contrast is
not primarily that of the visible lower world with
the invisible heavenly one, but of earth and the
heavens, the work of God's hands, that will be
changed (1 : 11–12), with the hoped for kingdom
that cannot be shaken (12 : 28). Vanhoye has written

---

[21] Vanhoye, 184.

an article[22] in which he shows that 'what cannot be
shaken' in 12:27 is probably the eschatological

[22] A. Vanhoye, 'L'*oikoumenē* dans l'epître aux Hébreux',
Biblica XLV (1964), 248–253. Vanhoye argues that the background
to 12:26–28 is not only to be found in Hag 2:6 quoted in
Heb 12:26 'Yet once more I will shake not only the earth but
also the heaven', but also in a whole series of texts from the
psalms and the prophets. Most important of these is Ps 96:10:
'Say among the nations, "The Lord reigns! yea, the world
(*oikoumenē*) is established, it shall never be moved (*ou
saleuthēsetai*)".' Vanhoye suggests that the words *ta mē
saleuomena*, 'the things that will not be moved' (RSV 'what
cannot be shaken'), in Heb 12:27 are an echo of 'it shall never
be moved' in the psalm: and that Hebrews 12:27 is, implicitly,
referring to the eschatological *oikoumenē*. He compares the
psalm with, among other texts, Is 62:4, which speaks of the
heavenly Jerusalem and her new *oikoumenē*: 'You shall no more
be termed Forsaken, and your land shall no more be termed
Desolate; but you shall be called My Will, and your land
Oikoumenē'. (I have adapted RSV in order to follow the Greek
literally.) Returning to the psalm Vanhoye comments: 'For anyone who bears in mind the distinction between the two eons, the
obvious interpretation is that the *oikoumenē* refers here to the
eon to come, the eschatological reality. This reality is brought
into being at the exaltation of Christ; the reader will recognise
an announcement of this in the ingressive aorist *ho Kurios
ebasileusen*, the Lord has assumed power, he has inaugurated
his kingdom (cf Dn 7:14).' Vanhoye is, of course, speaking of the
interpretation of the psalm as a messianic eschatological text by
early christians generally, and by the author of Hebrews in particular. These passages bring the new eschatological world, the
oikoumenē, into a close relationship with the eschatological
Jerusalem, the heavenly city that is to be identified, ultimately,
with the living community of the church, as in Revelation 21
and 22. Heb 12:26–28 does not speak of cosmology, though it
uses cosmological imagery, but of the eschatological community.
To quote Vanhoye once again: 'Through his Alexandrian forma-
tion the author of Hebrews was less tempted than anyone to
think of eschatological realities in a material fashion. He

world (*oikoumenē*), as clearly in 2:5 and, as Vanhoye suggests, in 1:6 also. If this suggestion is correct, then yet another hellenistic word, and one that
is clearly an equivalent of *aiōn*, as a comparison of
2:5 'the *oikoumene* to come' and 6:5 'the *aiōn* to
come' shows, is found to stand under the basically
eschatological thought-structure of Hebrews. The
aiōnes of both 11:3 and 1:2 are to be interpreted
along the line suggested by Westcott for 1:2: 'The
sum of the "periods of time" including all that is
manifested in and through them.' The visible
world is indeed a spatial one, but it is of its nature
transitory, shakeable, and must one day give place
to the unshakeable *oikoumenē*, kingdom and city of
God.

There remain only two occurrences of the word
aiōn to be considered, and these are both clearly
eschatological. Between them they establish very
neatly and fully the tension that characterises New
Testament eschatology. At 6:4–5 we read of members of the christian community as 'those who have
once been enlightened, who have tasted the heavenly
gift, and have become partakers of the Holy Spirit,
and have tasted the goodness of the word of God

---

conceives of it rather as spiritual community in which believers
are united with the saints and the angels, and in which they have
open access to God through Jesus (cf 12:22–24). In speaking of
it he loves to use the metaphors "house" (3:6; 10:21), "city"
(11:10, 16; 12:22; 13:14), "homeland" (11:14). There is nothing
extraordinary in the fact that he has taken up another word also
provided for him by the LXX: *oikoumenē*', *art cit*, 253.

and the powers of the age to come *(mellontos aiōnos)*'. This enlightenment may well be the effect of the sacrament of baptism, which is often called by the Greek Fathers simply 'enlightenment', *phōtismos*. The heavenly gift that is tasted is reminiscent of the 'bread from heaven' of Jn 6 : 31 following, which begins from the jewish tradition that the messiah, like Moses of old, would bring the heavenly gift of the manna, and goes on to present Jesus and his eucharistic flesh and blood as the true bread from heaven. The Holy Spirit is God's eschatological gift to his people, as in the text from Joel quoted in Ac 2 : 17ff: 'And in the last days it shall be, God declares, that I will pour out my Spirit upon all flesh, and your sons and your daughters shall prophesy, and your young men shall see visions, and your old men shall dream dreams; yea, and on my menservants and my maidservants in those days I will pour out my Spirit'. The word of God is here God's final eschatological word which he has spoken to us through his Son 'in these last days' (Heb 1 : 2). There is little room in such a context for Cambier's idea that 'to come' *(mellontos)* does not really mean to come; if these powers are already tasted they remain nevertheless truly the powers of the age to come, which are tasted only by way of anticipation now, and will be fully shared only when the age to come has fully arrived.

The same tension is clearly evident in 9 : 26: 'as it

is, he has appeared once for all at the end of the age (literally: "at the end of the ages", *epi sunteleia tōn aiōnōn*) to put away sin by the sacrifice of himself'. The ages have come to their end, as in 1:2 these days have come to their last (*ep' eschatou tōn hēmerōn toutōn*), but yet the age to come has not yet fully arrived: 'just as it is appointed for men to die once, and after that comes judgment, so Christ, having been offered once to bear the sins of many, will appear a second time, not to deal with sin but to save those who are eagerly waiting for him' (9:28). The authentic early christian note of waiting and watching for the parousia of Christ so that our salvation might be fulfilled is unmistakable here, nor does it seem, despite Moffatt's assessment, in any way foreign to the deeper thought of the author of Hebrews. Vanhoye's literary analysis of the epistle leads on to a study, in his final chapter, of the conceptual structure of Hebrews. He finds that each of the three sections of the central third part of the epistle and each paragraph of the central second section within this is given over predominantly to a sacrificial theme, to an ecclesiological theme, or to an eschatological one. Heb 9:11–28, the second half of the second section of the third part, the more important half since it is concerned with the fulfilment of the typology of the first half, is divided into three paragraphs, as we have seen: 9:11–14, 9:15–23 and 9:24–28. Now 9:11–14 is principally concerned with sacrifice, with the once for all entry into the Holy Place and the effectiveness of the blood of Christ who through the eternal Spirit offered himself to God. Heb 9:15–23 is concerned with the subject of the covenant, which is of course an ecclesiological theme; is not *the* covenant saying of the Old Testament 'I will be your God and you shall be my people'? Heb 9:23–28 is principally concerned with eschatology, both what has been realised already, the effective sacrifice once for all at the end of the age, and what still awaits realisation, the second coming of Christ. It is therefore in no way accidental or extraneous to the thought of Hebrews that the note of expectation of the parousia should appear at this point. The sign of realised eschatology in Hebrews is, very often, the appearance of the words 'once' and 'once for all'. Vanhoye notes that 'once' occurs three times in this short paragraph, in order to emphasise the unique event of the cross: Christ has appeared once (*hapax*; RSV 'once for all'), has died once (*hapax*) as all men do, and has been offered once (*hapax*).[23] Let us turn now to an examination of these two words.

At the conclusion of the Melchizedek chapter, and in preparation for the typological contrast be-

[23] Vanhoye's discussion of the pattern: sacrifice–ecclesiology–eschatology in 9:11–28 occurs on pp 238–239; his note on the triple repetition of *hapax* in 9:26–28 on p 159. At that point Vanhoye also takes note of the use of *ephapax* in 7:27 and 9:12, and of *hapax* in 9:7.

tween the levitical sacrifices and Christ's sacrifice in chapters 8–9, we are told: 'He has no need, like those high priests, to offer sacrifices daily, first for his own sins and then for those of the people; he did this once for all (*ephapax*) when he offered up himself. Indeed, the law appoints men in their weakness as high priests, but the word of the oath, which came later than the law, appoints a Son who has been made perfect for ever' (7:27–28). The emphatic 'once for all' emphasises the uniqueness of the Christ event in contrast with the daily sacrifices of the old law, and it is precisely because of this uniqueness that the Son has been perfected in his priesthood for ever. The eon of his priesthood has no end because it is both the eon to come and the last eon, inaugurated and anticipated in the decisive event of Calvary.

At 9:7 we read that the high priest, in contrast with the continual ministry in the outer tent, goes into the holy of holies 'but once (*hapax*) a year' with the blood of atonement. In fulfilment of this typology Christ 'entered once for all (*ephapax*) into the Holy Place, taking not the blood of goats and calves but his own blood, thus securing an eternal redemption' (9:12). The *hapax* of the high priest looks forward to the *ephapax*, the fuller form for emphasis by contrast, of Christ's self-offering. In 9:25–26 the contrast is stated in terms of 'repeatedly' and 'yearly' on the one hand and 'once' (*hapax*) on the other: 'Nor was it to offer himself repeatedly, as the high priest enters the Holy Place yearly with blood not his own; for then he would have had to suffer repeatedly since the foundation of the world. But as it is, he has appeared once for all (*hapax*) at the end of the age to put away sin by the sacrifice of himself.' Since the word *hapax* is not used of the high priest here, the simpler form suffices to bring out with a brusque emphasis the uniqueness of the Christ event. This is then hammered home with the repetition of *hapax* in the next two verses: Christ died once, Christ was offered once. There is one further use of the word *ephapax* in the context of offering at 10:10: 'And by that will we have been sanctified through the offering of the body of Jesus Christ once for all.' Here *ephapax* appears at the end of the sentence for additional emphasis. The idea is present also in the 'single sacrifice' and the 'single offering' of 10:12 and 14.

In dependence upon this one self-offering of Christ, the enlightenment, the tasting and the partaking of those who enter the christian community is something that happens once (6:4–5), just as at 10:2 it is implied that christians no longer have any consciousness of sin, since they have been cleansed once (*hapax*). Hebrews insists upon this point in order to exclude the possibility of apostasy, which seems to have been a real danger in the community which it is addressing (6:6).

Finally the eschatological shaking at the plenary

coming of the kingdom is naturally an unrepeatable event: 'now he has promised "Yet once more (*Eti hapax*) I will shake not only the earth but also the heaven". This phrase, "yet once more", indicates the removal of what is shaken, as of what has been made, in order that what cannot be shaken may remain. Therefore let us be grateful for receiving a kingdom that cannot be shaken' (12 : 26–28).

This should suffice to establish the thoroughgoing eschatology of the structure of thought in Hebrews. It remains to consider more closely the interconnection between typology and eschatology.

It is a paradox of the history of the interpretation of Hebrews that this letter which sets out so clearly to demonstrate the unique, realised eschatological character of the event of the cross should nevertheless, more than any other New Testament writing, not excluding St Matthew's gospel with its refrain 'All this took place to fulfil what the Lord had spoken by the prophet' (1 : 22 etc) and the statement 'Think not that I have come to abolish the law and the prophets; I have come not to abolish them but to fulfil them. For truly, I say to you, till heaven and earth pass away, not an iota, not a dot, will pass from the law until all is accomplished' (5 : 17–18), have been taken as showing a fundamental continuity between Old Testament institutions, in particular the systems of sacrifice and priesthood, and those of the New. A careful examination of what St Matthew

really means by 'fulfilment' would, I think, show
many of the typological and allegorical kinds of
imagery and transference of prophecy that we have
discovered in Hebrews; but that is not our present
concern. The literalising interpretation of Hebrews
has clearly been influenced by the evolving history
of the concept of the ministry of the church. This
was inevitable, sooner or later, once the word *hiereus*
was applied both to Christ and to the ministers of
the church; but through the patristic period this was
largely a matter of the co-existence of two pieces of
applied Old Testament typology that had a living
sense of biblical imagery.[24] It has often been suggested, eg by N. Lash, that the literalising and
paganising interpretation of the 'priesthood' of the
ministry, which would imply as its foundation a
literal priesthood of Christ, stems from the feudal
period: 'There should be no need to prove that a

---

[24] The classic patristic work on the christian ministry is, of
course, John Chrysostom's *De Sacerdotio.* (MG 48, 623ff.) In
book 3, paragraph 4, he writes to inculcate awe and reverence
for the ministerial office in his readers, making use of the splen-
dour of the high priest's robes as described in Leviticus, and then
applies this typologically to the eucharist: 'When you see the
Lord sacrificed and lying there, and the priest (some manuscripts
read "high priest") standing over the victim and praying, and
everyone scarlet with that most precious blood, do you still think
that you are among men, and standing upon the earth . . .?'
Chrysostom goes on to exploit the typology of the sacrifice of
Elijah on Mount Carmel, when the fire came down from heaven,
comparing it to the grace of God that comes down upon the
sacrament and inflames the hearts of the participants.

bishop is not a superior class of being, belonging to a superior class of christians, because the structures and consciousness of the church should be such as to prevent the thought ever entering our heads. It has only been able to enter our heads because, in the past, the episcopate has too often been exercised and understood as a social role, definable in terms of pagan or Old Testament priesthood viewed through the prism of feudal political theory.'[25] Lash is perhaps right in seeing the seeds of clericalism in the mediaeval period, but it is possible also that so far as the theologians are concerned, at least, the instinctive patristic grasp of typology remained a major force in exegesis and in the construction of *summas* and *compendia* throughout the mediaeval period.[26] But in any case the primary theological question is about the nature of the priesthood of Christ, for contemporary theology has come to see very clearly that the ministers of the church are 'priests' only in so far as they are min-

[25] N. Lash, 'Priest or presbyter', in *Authority in a changing Church*, London 1968, 93.

[26] Too often it is forgotten that the work of full master in theology, throughout the mediaeval period, was that of the *magister in sacra pagina*, who lectured day by day upon the scriptures, taking up the problems that arose from the text into the theological *quaestiones*. See M. D. Chenu, *Introduction à l'étude de Saint Thomas d'Aquin*, Paris 1950, 207–212. St Thomas' *quaestio* on the priesthood of Christ in the *Summa Theologiae* (IIIa. 22) makes a much fuller use of biblical theology than has been customary in our theological manuals.

isters and instruments of the unique priesthood of Christ which cannot be passed on to others.[27]

[27] See eg J. Colson, *Ministre de Jésus-Christ ou le sacerdoce de l'évangile*, Paris 1966, 344: 'The epistle to the Hebrews, vigorously declaring that the risen Jesus has a priesthood (*hierosunē*) which is not passed on (*aparabaton*), not transmitted to others, does not wish to deny the possibility that the unique eternal Priest will make his ministers in the Church, in so far as they are his instruments, sharers in his *hierosunē*. This merely underlines the originality of the priestly function in christianity as compared with the Jewish and pagan priesthoods.

The same may be said of the refusal (ie in the New Testament and the primitive church, as the subtitle of Colson's book shows: "A study of the priestly character of christian ministers in the primitive church") to give the title of *hiereis* to christian ministers.

This refusal, in fact, is not intended as a denial of the priestly character of their ministry, but to avoid confusing it with that of the *hiereis* of the old covenant. Once again, this brings out the wholly original character of the priestly function of the ministers of the new covenant, both in comparison with the Jewish priesthood and *a fortiori* with pagan priesthoods. The christian ministry is fundamentally, essentially *apostolic*, and as such is merely a *function*, an *instrumentality*, a "sacramentalisation" of the only effective *hiereus*: Christ the Redeemer whose death and Resurrection the minister proclaims and actualises in ritual.'

I have reservations about the propriety of the use of the word 'actualise' there, it is a little too close to M. Fraeyman's 'repeat' and 'fulfil' for comfort; and does not St Paul regard the eucharist as precisely a *proclamation* of the Lord's death? (1 Cor 11:26). This apart, what Colson is saying with a much fuller foundation in New Testament exegesis comes close to what Thomas Aquinas said so succinctly 700 years ago: 'Christ, however, is the source of all priesthood: for the priesthood of the law was a prefiguration of his; and a priest of the new law acts in his name (*in persona ipsius operatur*), according to 2 Cor 2:10: "What I have given, if I have given anything, was for you in Christ's name".' 111a. 22. 4. c. From the conclusion reached in this essay, it is in the typological 'priesthood' of Christ that his ministers share.

Our basic concern is with this priesthood, as this is revealed to us in the enigmatic, allegorical typology of Hebrews. It is the contention of this chapter that the enigma is directly related to eschatology: the Christ event, in its uniqueness, has inexhaustible depths of meaning, and this meaning is most fully bodied forth, not in the abstractions of philosophical theology but in the rich suggestiveness of typology. Symbolism has its own truth and its own precision. The imagery of Ps 139 stands in striking contrast with philosophico-theological statements about the divine omnipresence, but it cannot be claimed that this symbolism lacks precision or fails to state anything: 'Whither shall I go from thy Spirit? Or whither shall I flee from thy presence? If I ascend to heaven, thou art there! If I make my bed in Sheol, thou art there! If I take the wings of the morning and dwell in the uttermost parts of the sea, even there thy hand shall lead me, and thy right hand shall hold me. If I say "Let only darkness cover me, and the day about me be night", even the darkness is not dark to thee, the night is bright as the day; for darkness is as light with thee.'

The imagery of Hebrews is perhaps not as successful poetically as the profound and moving beauty of that psalm, but it has intellectual precision and power, and a unified viewpoint mirrored in the complicated close weave of the literary structure, and certainly no lack of the capacity to make definite affirmations. Nowhere are these affirmations more forceful than in the passages concerning the uniqueness and unrepeatableness of the event of the cross. One great advantage in reading the theme of priesthood in Hebrews as a sustained and unified piece of allegorical typology from first to last, if this reading is correct, is that it allows the full force of the eschatological affirmations to come through with an untrammelled emphasis. To adopt and adapt a phrase from dialectical theology, it allows God's action in Christ to be truly God's definitive action: it lets the *hapax* be *hapax*.

5
Conclusion

In these few concluding pages I shall not be concerned with summing up what I have said already; the confrontation between typology and eschatology at the end of the last chapter necessarily provided, at the same time, a restatement of what we have found typology and eschatology to be in Hebrews. In conclusion I wish briefly to indicate some possible conclusions for New Testament theology as a whole as also for dogmatic theology.

It has been argued above that Hebrews is a seamless robe woven from beginning to end throughout, both in terms of typological symbolism and in terms of literary structure, the one mirroring the other. If this is so, is not the constantly reiterated attempt to dissect Hebrews and lift out from it a literal definition or conception of Christ's priesthood an operation of a particularly delicate and perilous nature? It will be replied that we are entitled to do this because of the many other indications in the New Testament that point to Christ's literal priesthood. It is to this argument I now turn. It is impossible here to examine all the sacrificial and possibly priestly texts in the New Testament, a whole book would be necessary for that and a nearly infinite amount of reading and study. All I can hope to do here, principally through an examination of M. Barth's most interesting paper *Was Christ's death a sacrifice?*, is to indicate the kind of argument used in works written from this kind of standpoint and to establish the legitimacy, in this way, of raising the question afresh.

One point must be made, or rather remade, at the start: one cannot in fact securely argue from sacrifice to priesthood, though this is in fact what Barth and many other writers do. In the levitical view of priesthood expressed in the priestly source (and this is only one Old Testament view of priesthood) one may argue from priesthood to sacrifice, and there is a tendency visible to subordinate to this the sacrificial activities of others, as for example in the transformation of the old family sacrifice of passover into a part of the sacrificial liturgy of the Jerusalem temple and its priesthood. But it remains impossible to argue from the bare fact of sacrifice to the possession of priesthood. Yet this is just what is done by, for example, J. Coppens:

Let us note to start with that there is no need to
search out whether priestly ideas were present in
Jesus' mind. If the question is asked in that way
the answer cannot be negative, if one thinks only
of the institution of the eucharist. It is true that
the discussions about the setting of the Last
Supper, Passover supper or *haburah* supper, and
over the meaning of the words spoken by Christ,
are not concluded. But all the same there is a tendency to general agreement over the authentic
existence of an allusion to the blood of the covenant. Therefore the sacrificial character of the
ritual of the Last Supper is certain, and consequently the priestly attitude taken up by Jesus
there is solidly established.[1]

It is striking that Coppens does not even raise the
question of Jesus' words and actions, in the starkly
simple family ritual over the bread and the wine
which are all that the gospels record from the supper,
being possibly a piece of symbolic typology in which
he interpreted, and left an effective memorial of, his
death for the apostles and for the church. To mere
assertion one has the right of reply with a contrary
assertion. Further, the argument from covenant sacrifice to priesthood simply does not hold: Abraham

[1] J. Coppens, 'Le messianisme sacerdotal dans les écrits du
Nouveau Testament', in *La venue du Messie*, Recherches
Bibliques VI, Paris 1962, 105.

is patriarch, not priest, in the covenant sacrifice of Gn 15. And the description of the covenant-making at Sinai contains no reference to priesthood: Moses was not a priest, though later jewish tradition turned him into one, Aaron is at this time merely one of the elders of Israel, and the young men commissioned to do the actual killing are nowhere described as priests, and indeed 'young men' would be a rather odd way of referring to priests. And above all, even if it were possible, and I do not think it is, to establish an argument from covenant sacrificer to priest in the Old Testament, how can we be sure of the propriety of this argument in the case of Jesus of Nazareth, the prophet who said: 'The sabbath was made for man, not man for the sabbath; so the Son of man is Lord even of the sabbath' (Mk 2 : 27–28), and: 'Hear me, all of you, and understand: there is nothing outside a man which by going into him can defile him; but the things which come out of a man are what defile him' (Mk 7 : 14–15), and time and again: 'You have heard that it was said to the men of old. . . . But I say to you . . .' (Mt 5), and: 'Go and learn what this means, "I desire mercy, and not sacrifice". For I came not to call the righteous, but sinners' (Mt 9 : 13). In view of these and like sayings of Jesus, which reveal his extraordinary freedom in dealing with the law, it is surely dangerous to presume that we know what Jesus' attitude would be with regard to traditional conceptions. If Jesus did think of the last supper as interpretative of his death as a literal covenant sacrifice, which I take leave to doubt, might not the layman and prophet from Nazareth have been appealing, implicitly, to pre-levitical ideas and situations? One cannot in any way regard Coppens' theory as proven.

M. Barth's paper[2] begins, in the first chapter, with a general survey of New Testament sacrificial texts, goes on, chapter two, to examine a selection of Old Testament passages, with special attention to sacrificial stories, eg Gn 15 and 22, continues in chapter 3 with an examination of Paul, John and the synoptics, then summarises his findings and tries to draw some conclusions in his concluding chapter. He does not examine Hebrews directly, but states that his treatment of the other New Testament passages was at least strongly influenced by Hebrews' account of the death of Christ.[3] His point about the importance of the Old Testament sacrificial stories for an understanding of its conception of sacrifice is well made; it cannot be said, however, that the final account of sacrifice, and in particular of the sacrifice of Christ which is *the* sacrifice,[4] is at all satisfactory:

Some Old Testament sacrifices, and some of the New Testament texts dealing with Jesus Christ's

[2] M. Barth, *Was Christ's death a sacrifice?*, Scottish Journal of Theology Occasional Papers no 9, Edinburgh-London 1961.
[3] M. Barth, 47, n 1.
[4] M. Barth, 48.

death as a sacrifice, agree in fundamental respects. They show that sacrifice is (1) Revelation and (2) Gift of God; (3) Service and (4) Intercession of a Faithful Servant before God; (5) Righteous Judgment and (6) Constitutive Action by God in favour of the People. Sacrifice includes and comprehends the 'motifs' of miraculous manifestation, obedience (to death) offered by a representative person, and of constitution of a community by judicial action. The term 'ordeal' (*Gottes-Urteil*) seems to be most fitting for defining the common denominator of all these elements and motifs. God, the Servant, and the people are inseparably united when a pleasing sacrifice takes place.[5]

This will not do at all as an account of the biblical idea of sacrifice. With the possible exception of miraculous manifestation, there is nothing whatever to discriminate between the life, intercession and death of Jeremiah the prophet and the literal and ritual sacrifices of the Old Testament and the Jerusalem temple in the time of Jesus. Barth tries to make amends by introducing what he calls a 'limitation' to this description (there are two other limitations):

> Neither the concept of an ordeal nor the elaboration of its various aspects can be exhaustive. For

[5] M. Barth, 46.

in the Bible sacrifice can also be called, or described, as a gift *to* God ('offering'). And the blood poured out in sacrifice can almost animistically be identified with 'life' (Lv 17:10–12; Dt 12:23ff; cf Jn 19:34; 6:51–58). To discard the respective texts by discrediting them as primitive, inferior, ultimately pagan residues, and to jump to the higher, 'sublimated' motifs of faithful service, justification by grace, constitution of community— this is to refuse to face the actuality of the Bible and the challenge to more and deeper theological thinking contained in it.[6]

This latter point is well made, but Barth seems to have no inkling of how close he has come to doing that himself; if they are not primitive, inferior and pagan aspects of sacrifice for him, they are markedly secondary in his presentation, thus failing to correct the central description which is unrecognisable as an account of the sacrifices of the bible. The reason is not far to seek; Barth is determined to wrest a univocal, or a literally analogical that is as near to the univocal as possible, concept of sacrifice that will cover as many uses of the word (or words, eg *asham*, sacrifice for sin in Is 53:10) as possible. He makes a rigid and questionable distinction between the 'cultic character of Christ's sacrifice' and the 'ethical character' of the spiritual sacrifices of

[6] M. Barth, 46.

the apostles and other christians.[7] Yet it seems certain
that the 'sacrifice' of the servant of Yahweh is a fundamental clue to an understanding of the sacrifice
('sacrifice'?) of Jesus in the New Testament
generally, and with all probability for his own understanding too. Barth has earlier, and with some exag-
geration, pointed to the priestly and sacrificial motifs
in the fourth servant song, but without realising
that mere enumeration cannot show whether one is
dealing with a piece of biblical typology or with a
sober description of literal fact. I cannot find any
real evidence in Barth that the servant, who may
well be simply the people of the Fall and Exile, is
literally a priest or literally offered in sacrifice. May
not what is true of the servant be true also of Jesus?
May it not be that a typological reading of the 'sacrifice' of the cross will in the end do the fullest
justice to the real meaning of the texts, to the
uniqueness of the Christ event, to the sheer mystery
of God's action at the cross?

Barth's real concern in trying to prove the literal
sacrifice of the cross emerges clearly on an earlier
page where he is discussing Harnack's view, and in a
footnote in which he indicates his disagreement with
Bultmann and Lohse: 'A. v. Harnack speaks for
many when he accepts the name "sacrifice" for
Christ's death only if it means nothing else than
(a) that by the cross the Old Testament's and

[7] M. Barth, 49.

Judaism's bloody sacrifices are factually terminated, (b) that the suffering of the pure and just man was accepted as containing saving features, (c) that injustice deserves punishment, and that a good man's death puts evildoers to shame and thus has a purifying effect', and 'Here and there a somehow sublimated view of Jesus Christ the (Socratic, Maccabean, Stoic or Existentialist) martyr removes the offence of sacrifice—of *the* real and true sacrifice which God has brought. When that obstacle is removed, the door is opened for an existentialist or moralist understanding of faith in Christ. Neither Bultmann nor Lohse fails to enter this door.'[8] The 'saving features' of Harnack are ultimately moralist because it is by his example alone that Jesus 'saves' us; and the existentialist account of the effectiveness of the cross is in terms of a change in one's self-understanding. Barth rightly looks for a statement of God's action in the event of the cross that transforms effectively and objectively man's standing before God. The language of sacrifice and expiation points to the real forgiveness of sins and atonement with God.

This is true, but it remains true even if we take all the priestly and sacrificial language as biblical symbol. Something of infinite mystery and value happens at the cross, God in Christ reconciles the world to himself through the one single perfect act of love and goodness performed by a man who is

[8] M. Barth, 11–12 and 43, footnote 2 of p 42.

identically, personally the Son of God. Its value is infinite since it is God's act and the human action of God made man; it has no limit on the human side since there is no possible way of sharing in the misery of human existence more fully, more generously than this: 'Greater love has no man than this, that a man lay down his life for his friends' (Jn 15:13). The language of sacrifice, expiation and priesthood points directly to this mystery of God's saving action; it does this no less effectively if it is interpreted, as I think it is rightly interpreted, as one of the great biblical images. The true scandal of the cross is not that it was literally a sacrifice, rather than symbolically one, but that it was the crucifixion of Christ, the crucifixion of the Lord of glory, as the context of 1 Cor 1–2 shows. The forgiveness and the atonement effected at the cross are mediated to us through the simple rituals of baptism and the eucharist, when these are received in faith; that the event from which the (seven) sacraments of the church derive their power is itself *literally* cultic, sacrificial and priestly is in no way evident.

Vanhoye has stated this point very clearly: 'Nor is Jesus said to have offered a sacrifice except in later texts (Eph 5:2; cf Gal 2:20), for the death of Jesus had nothing ritual about it: externally it was a political and judicial event, not a liturgical one. There was no cultic connotation, but bare historical reality. Its value depends upon no external cere-

7

mony, but upon the way in which Jesus personally takes the reality of this event: in obedience towards God (Mt 26 : 39) and in love towards us.'[9] Vanhoye's formulation leaves open just the possibility that Jesus' death is in some purely internal way a liturgical event[10]; this is the standpoint of those who understand the death of Christ as a spiritual sacrifice, but interpret 'spiritual' in a literalising, not in the johannine way. Provided that one is not trying to evacuate the mystery in rationalistic fashion, but to respect, rather, the mysterious eschatological saving action of God, the typological reading of the priestly and sacrificial language of the New Testament seems to me ultimately the one most faithful to the meaning of the texts.

With this brief critique of M. Barth's paper I have

[9] A. Vanhoye, *art cit*, 'De Christologia...', *Verbum Domini* XLIII (1965), 57.

[10] This is at first sight what St Thomas does in *S Th* IIIa. 22. 2 ad 2: 'To the second objection I reply that the killing of the man Christ can be related to two voluntary decisions. First, to the decision of the executioners; and then it does not have the character of a sacrifice (*hostia*), for Christ's killers are not said to have offered a sacrifice to God, but to have sinned most grievously. And the impious sacrifices of the gentiles, in which they sacrificed men to idols, bear the likeness of that sin. Secondly, the killing of Christ can be considered in relation to the will of the sufferer, who voluntarily offered himself in his passion; and on this side it has the character of a sacrifice'.

In respect of this text I would ask in all seriousness: is St Thomas literalising, or is he saving the appearances of the biblical typology? If he is literalising, I cannot follow him in so far as this is offered as interpretation of the New Testament.

tried to show the need for a reassessment of the sacrificial texts of the New Testament on the basis of the reinterpretation of Hebrews offered in this essay. And, of course, the other New Testament texts, and in particular the earlier and more basic ones, should be interpreted in their own terms, not in those of Hebrews. Now let us ask what consequences our findings, if true, would have for dogmatic theology.

First, it is not at all evident at first sight that dogmatic theology may not rightfully construct its own abstract and literal concepts of priesthood and sacrifice in which to interpret the mystery of God's action at the cross. I do not at all share the attitude of biblical scholars like O. Cullmann who finds a fundamental incompatibility between the 'essence' concepts of Greek philosophical thinking and the dynamic functional pattern of New Testament thought, particularly in christology.[11] But each theological enterprise carries within it its own peculiar risks and dangers, and I should like to point to those threatening here.

It has normally been presupposed, in the immense dogmatic and devotional literature on priesthood, that St Thomas is concerned, in his question on the priesthood of Christ in the *Summa*, to construct just

---

[11] See, in particular, Cullmann's work already cited, *The Christology of the New Testament*. And in criticism of Cullmann see J. Barr, *Old and New in interpretation*, 46, and the chapter 'Athens or Jerusalem?—The question of distinctiveness' for a discussion of the whole problem.

such an abstract, dogmatic idea of priesthood. I am not at all sure of the correctness of this interpretation. I have already pointed to the full use of biblical passages made in this question; I wonder whether St Thomas is not drawing on the whole biblical and patristic tradition, with its rich profusion of typological thinking, and ordering this with his characteristic emphasis on what is clear and rational, while fully respecting the typology and the mystery? It is not, in any case, to my purpose to attempt an exegesis of the *Summa* here; let us take rather this much simpler example of dogmatic construction, offered by an exegete writing as a dogmatician: 'No one would dream of contradicting the fact that the doctrine of the incarnation, that is to say, the fact and the belief that divine and human nature are united in the person of Jesus, gives us the right to acknowledge in our Saviour, a *priestly* mediator, the ideal, perfect example of such a mediator.'[12]

In the short passage from J. Coppens it is quite evident that the description of priesthood in Heb 5 : 1 is being put to work, together with the conception of Christ the mediator in 1 Tim 2 : 5, without regard to the context in either epistle, and with a mere supposition that 'mediatorship' may be identified with priestly appointment on behalf of men in relation to God. The context in 1 Timothy speaks of saving, redeeming and witnessing—and none of

[12] J. Coppens, 109.

these are priestly or cultic words. Coppens is not, therefore, offering us exegesis, he is engaged in the task of theological conceptual construction, a perfectly legitimate enterprise. But there is one special danger in building literal univocal or analogical concepts of priesthood and sacrifice. In theory analogical thinking allows for the possibility of an infinite distance between beings that are brought under the one concept (or is it a family of concepts?), as happens in all our speech about God. When we say that God is good or God is true, or simply that God exists, we are taking concepts familiar to us in our thinking about the world and ourselves in the world and projecting them outwards (and inwards: 'God is nearer to me than the most intimate part of myself'[13]) into the infinity of God where we no longer know what we mean, though we know we have to say these things. But these are all values, the 'pure perfections' of scholastic theology, that do not include in their meaning any reference to limitation and imperfection. But 'priesthood' and 'sacrifice' are not values, they are human institutions and offices, very much involved in the ambiguity and sinfulness and self-calculation of humanity, as the prophets, and Jesus following the

[13] 'Deus intimius intimo meo' in the famous phrase from Augustine. St Thomas says much the same in his more abstract and general way, probably echoing Augustine: 'Deus sit in omnibus rebus, et intime' (1a. 8. 1. c).

prophets, pointed out most forcefully. There will always be a danger, in thinking of Jesus as literally a priest, and of his death on the cross as literally a sacrifice, mediated to us as they are through the sacraments, of coming to count on our own sacramental activity in the way denounced by the prophets, and of allowing this to colour our view of the event of the cross itself, to lose the sense of discontinuity with all human strivings that goes along with the continuity. The theological work of concept building, then, is not illegitimate in this field, but a fuller realisation of the underlying biblical typology is preferable.

With that penultimate sentence of the last paragraph we have reached explicitly the question implicit in this whole essay: continuity or discontinuity with the Old Testament priesthood, and through that, in a more limited way, with pagan priesthoods generally. Since the full-blown sacrificial system of Israel was in large measure taken over from the Canaanites, though with a considerable conceptual transformation, there is a definite link between Old Testament priesthood and sacrifice and that revealed to us in the study of comparative religion. But what of the continuity or discontinuity between Old and New Testament? My answer to this question has been implicit upon each page of this essay, and especially in the confrontation between typology and eschatology attempted at the end of the last chapter.

Let us begin from a statement by C. K. Barrett that seems to me eminently balanced and accurate: '. . . there is in fact no writing in the New Testament which emphasises more strongly than Hebrews the inadequacy of the Old Testament and its institutions, and the discontinuity (as well as continuity) between the testaments'.[14] This statement is made in Barrett's essay on the eschatology of Hebrews which we have already seen. This point seems significant: it is when one gives full value to the eschatological

[14] C. K. Barrett, 'The eschatology of the Epistle to the Hebrews', 382. Compare with this O. Michel's more dialectical statement (quoted by J. Bonsirven at p 372, n 1 of his commentary): 'one finds everywhere, in the gospels as in the Pauline writings, an absolute Yes and an absolute No with regard to the content of the old covenant. The Messiah, the cross of Jesus, the new covenant put an end to the old one and yet fulfil its deepest meaning. No set of words formulates better than this the tension between the suppression and the fulfilment in defining the relationship of the New Testament to the Old.'

Vanhoye is more systematic, not to say more mathematical: 'Because of this, a comparison of the two phases establishes three kinds of relationship: likeness, difference, and superiority. We can sum up these three relationships in one word: fulfilment (cf Mt 5 : 17 and Rm 13 : 10), but one should note that the author of the epistle never uses *plērōma* and *plēroun*. The New Testament fulfils the Old, that is to say, (i) in one sense it continues it, corresponds to it, resembles it; (ii) in another sense, it marks a break, it is different, it replaces it; (iii) in yet another sense, it dominates over it, it is incomparably superior to it' (p 249).

Perhaps neither of these two formulations, useful as far as they go, gives full value to the fact that Hebrews refrains quite deliberately from saying that the New Testament fulfils or perfects the Old. The Old, law and priesthood together, is changed (7 : 12), set aside (7 : 18), abolished (10 : 9).

element in Hebrews that the fundamental discontinuity that underlies the very real continuity is most securely grasped. It is clear that the Old Testament and the tradition that sprang from it formed the particular, local, historical world into which Jesus of Nazareth was born. In a very real sense the whole of Old Testament revelation and history leads up to that moment, sometimes directly and positively, sometimes indirectly and more negatively. Not only is a people and an historical situation prepared and blessed, in part, for the coming of Christ: the Old Testament provides also the primary conceptual and linguistic (and these two are all but identically one, as always) situation into which Jesus was born and the Palestinian, and still in a fundamental sense the hellenistic, church was to work and think. Old Testament sayings and events are the primary tools for understanding the mystery of Christ from end to end of the New Testament. There is thus a very real measure of continuity, and this also in this matter of the priestly and sacrificial understanding of the mystery of the event at the cross. But there is a saying of Jesus about the impossibility of putting new wine into old leathers that forever forbids us to forget the even more radical discontinuity between the institutions of the Old Testament, man-made in large part, however much they were blessed by God for their own time and their own place, and the gospel event itself, which takes place in human flesh and blood, but which is primarily God's gift to us, the revelation of a love that shatters our human world: 'God so loved the world that he gave his only Son' (Jn 3:16). Hebrews has a very vivid apprehension of the full humanity of Jesus; was it not in the days of his flesh that he offered up prayers and supplications (5:7)? And yet the discontinuity and uniqueness of the Christ-event are brought out with unparalleled force: the law made nothing perfect (7:19), while Christ has appeared once for all at the end of the age to put away sin by the sacrifice of himself (9:26). Hebrews teaches us unmistakably that any statement of the relationship between Old Testament and New that fails to bring out the discontinuity underlying the continuity is unfaithful to the new creation in Christ.

There is one final affirmation to be made. The thesis argued in this essay may seem, superficially, to have something in common with contemporary endeavours to *demythologise* the New Testament. I am not without sympathy with some of the work that R. Bultmann and others have tried to carry out under this rubric, though one must question the usefulness of the description. In any case, the argument of this essay moves towards remythologisation, or, in a phrase dependent upon J. Moffat, towards turning the literal, because literalised, back into the figurative. If one takes the biblical figures and symbols with the seriousness and sympathy that they call for, one will have no difficulty in acknowledging in the typology of Hebrews an indispensable part of New Testament revelation, indeed of the full Christ-event itself.[15] I am deeply convinced that if we are ready to look at Hebrews with fresh eyes, not forgetting our church traditions but remembering the best in them, those elements by which we are truly bound, we will find in Hebrews a meeting place for faith, in its irreplaceable statement of what God has, once for all, done for us in Christ.

[15] C. Ernst, 'Priesthood and ministry', *New Blackfriars*, XLIX, 571 (December 1967), 124: 'The theological idiom of the author of the Epistle to the Hebrews provides us with what was called above an 'interpretation' of the dynamic transcendence of the Christ-Event. To speak of interpretation is to recognise the possibility of alternative interpretations; it is not to suggest that alternative interpretations are open to us today as a matter of free choice. The priestly and cultic interpretation of Christ in Hebrews is one of those inspired and canonical interpretations of Christ which, together with, say, the Johannine and Pauline interpretations, help to constitute the very reality of Christ himself in his communicable meaning. The Epistle to the Hebrews, inspired as we believe it to be by the Spirit of Christ, is an intrinsic element in the mystery of Christ; such that *no* communication of Christ to christians is possible which may not be interpreted in priestly and cultic terms. . . .'

Bibliography

Abbreviations

NTS   New Testament Studies.

TWNT   Theologisches Wörterbuch zum Neuen Testament (Stuttgart 1933–).

BAMBERG C., ' "Melchisadech'. Erbe und Auftrag', *Benediktinische Monatschrift* 40 (1964), 5–21

BARR J., *Old and New in interpretation*, London 1966

BARRETT C.K., 'The eschatology of the Epistle to the Hebrews', in *The background of the New Testament and its eschatology*, ed W. D. Davies and D. Daube, Cambridge 1956

BARROIS A., 'Le sacrifice du Christ au Calvaire', *Revue des Sciences Philosophiques et Théologiques* XIV (1925), 145–166

BARTH M., 'The Old Testament in Hebrews', in *Current issues in New Testament interpretation*, ed W. Klassen and G. F. Sneider, London 1926, 53–78, 263–273

—— *Was Christ's death a sacrifice?* Scottish Journal of Theology Occasional Papers no 9, Edinburgh–London 1961

BEHM J., *Thuō, thusia, thusiastērion*, TWNT III, 180–190

BENOIT P., 'La plénitude de sens des livres saints', *Revue Biblique* LXVII (1960), 161–196

BERTETTO D., 'La natura del sacerdozio secondo Heb 5 1–4 e le sue realizzazioni nel Nuovo Testamento, *Salesianum* XXVI (1964), 395–440

BEST E., 'Spiritual sacrifice. General priesthood in the New Testament', *Interpretation* XIV (1960), 273–299

BETZ O., 'Le ministère cultuel dans la secte de Qumran et dans le christianisme primitif', in *La secte de Qumran et les origines du christianisme* Récherches Bibliques 4, Louvain 1959, 162–202

BONSIRVEN J., *Epître aux Hébreux*, Verbum Salutis, Paris 1943

—— 'Le sacerdoce et le sacrifice de Jésus-Christ d'après l'épître aux Hébreux', *Nouvelle Revue Théologique* LXVI (1939), 641–660, 769–786

BOURGIN C., 'Le Christ-prêtre et la purification des péchés selon l'épître aux Hébreux', *Lumière et Vie* XXXVI (1958), 67–90

—— 'Le sang du Christ et le culte spirituel', Heb 9. 11–15, *Assemblées du Seigneur* XXXIV (1963), 26–53

BRADY C., 'The world to come in the Epistle to the Hebrews', *Worship* XXXIX (1965), 329–339

BROWN R. E., 'The history and development of a theory of a *sensus plenior*', *Catholic Biblical Quarterly* XV (1953), 141–162

—— 'The *sensus plenior* in the last ten years', *Catholic Biblical Quarterly* XXV (1963), 262–285

BROWNLEE W. H., 'Messianic motifs of Qumran and the New Testament', NTS III (1953), 195–210

BRUCE F. F., *The Epistle to the Hebrews*, London 1964

—— ' "To the Hebrews" or "To the Essenes" ', NTS IX (1963), 217–232

BÜCHSEL F., *Die Christologie des Hebräerbriefes*, Gütersloh 1922

BULTMANN R., 'Ursprung und Sinn der Typologie als hermeneutischer Methode', *Theologische Literaturzeitung* (1950), 205–212

CAMBIER J., 'Eschatologie ou Hellénisme dans l'épître aux Hébreux, *Salesianum* XI (1949), 62–96

CASSERLEY J. V. L., 'Event symbols and myth symbols', *Anglican Theological Review* XXXVIII (1956), 127–137, 242–248

CATALUCCI E., 'Hoi proserchomenoi tō theō', *Studio teologico del verbo 'proserchomenoi' nella lettera agli Ebrei*, Rome 1956 (Gregorian dissertation)

CERFAUX L., 'Le sacré du Grand-prêtre d'après Héb 5. 5–10', *Bible et Vie Chrétienne* XXI (1958), 54–58

CLARKSON E., 'The antecedents of the High Priest theme in Hebrews', *Anglican Theological Review* XXIX (1947), 92ff

CLAVIER H., 'Ho logos tou theou dans l'épître aux Hébreux', in Davies-Daube (eds), *The background of the New Testament and its eschatology*, Cambridge 1956, 81–93

CODY A., *Heavenly sanctuary and liturgy in the Epistle to the Hebrews*, St Meinrad 1960

COPPENS J., 'Le messianisme sacerdotal dans les écrits du Nouveau Testament', *La venue du Messie*, Recherches Bibliques 6, Louvain 1962, 101–112

——, 'Le problème de sens bibliques', *Concilium* XXX (1967), 107–118

—— 'Les affinités qumrániennes de l'épître aux Hébreux', *Nouvelle Revue Théologique*, LXXXIV (1962), 128–141, 257–282

—— *Les harmonies des deux Testaments*, Tournai-Paris 1949

COSTANZO G., *Il peccato e la sua remissione nella lettera agli Ebrei*, Rome 1964 (Gregorian dissertation)

COSTE J., 'Notion grecque et notion biblique de la "souf-france éducatrice". A propos de Heb 5. 7–8', *Recherches de Science Religieuse* XLIII (1955), 481–523

CULLMANN O., *Christ and time*, 2nd Eng edn, London 1962
—— *The Christology of the New Testament*, Eng edn, London 1959

DA DELICETTO G., 'Salvezza perfetta e redenzione oggettiva nella lettera agli Ebrei', *Laurentianum* (1960), 417–434

DAHL N.A., 'A new and living way. The approach to God according to Hebrews 10:19–25', *Interpretation* V (1951), 403ff

DANIÉLOU J., *From shadows to reality*, Eng edn, London 1960

DE JONGE M. and VAN DER WOUDE A. S., 'Melchizedek and the New Testament', NTS XII (1966), 301–326

DEL MEDICO H. E., 'Melchisédec', *Zeitschrift für die alt-testamentiche Wissenschaft* LXIX (1957), 160–170

DELPORTE L., 'Les principes de la typologie biblique et les eléments figuratifs du sacrifice de l'expiation', *Ephemerides Theologiae Lovanienses* III (1926), 307–327

DE LUBAC H., 'A propos de l'allégorie chrétienne', *Recherches de Science Religieuse* XLVII (1959), 5–43

—— 'Typologie et allégorisme', *Recherches de Science Religieuse* XXXIV (1947), 180–226

DE ROSA P., *Il concetto di Aiônios nell'epistula agli Ebrei. Contributo alla teologia del Nuovo Testamento*, Rome 1956 (Gregorian dissertation)

DESCAMPS A., 'La structure de l'épître aux Hébreux', *Revue diocésaine de Tournai* IX (1954), 251–288, 333–338.

—— 'Le sacerdoce du Christ d'après l'épître aux Hébreux', *Revue diocésaine de Tournai* IX (1954), 429–434, 529–534

—— 'Notes sur le sacrifice et le sacerdoce dans l'Ecriture', *Revue diocésaine de Tournai* IX (1954), 23–28

DIBELIUS M., 'Der himmlische Kultus nach dem Hebräer-brief', *Theologische Blätter* (1942), 1ff

DILLENSCHNEIDER C., *Le Christ l'unique prêtre et nous ses prêtres*, 2 vols, Paris 1961

DIMMLER E., *Melchisedec. Gedanken über das Hohepriester-tum Christi nach den Hebräerbrief*, Kampen 1921

DU PLESSIS P. J., *Teleios: The idea of perfection in the New Testament*, Kampen 1959

ERNST C., 'Priesthood and ministry', *New Blackfriars* XLIX (1967), 121–132

ESTEVE H. M., *De caelesti mediatione sacerdotali Christi juxta Heb 8:3–4*, Madrid 1949

FANNON P., 'The Dutch catechism: its hidden persuaders', *Clergy Review* (1968), 3–13

FEUILLET A., 'La demeure céleste et la destinée des chrétiens', *Recherches de Science Religieuse* XLIV (1956), 160–192, 360–402

—— 'Les points de vue nouveaux dans l'eschatologie de l'épître aux Hébreux', *Studia Evangelica* II (1964), 369–387

FILSON F. V., *'Yesterday.' A study of Hebrews in the light of chapter 13*, London 1967

FITZMYER J., ' "Now this Melchizedek..." Heb 7:1; Ps 110:4; Gn 14:8ff', *Catholic Biblical Quarterly* XXV (1963), 305–321

FRAEYMAN M., 'La spiritualisation de l'idée du Temple dans les épîtres pauliniennes', *Ephemerides Theologiae Lovanienses* XXIII (1947), 378–412

FRANSEN I., 'Jésus pontife parfait du parfait sanctuaire', *Bible et Vie Chrétienne* XX (1957), 79–91

FRIEDRICH G., 'Das Lied vom Hohenpriester in Zusammenhang von Heb 4:4–5:10', *Theologische Zeitung* XVIII (1962), 95–115

GAIDE G., 'Jésus le prêtre unique, Heb. 4: 10–10: 25', *Evangile* LIII (1964), 5–72

GALOPIN P. M., 'Le sacerdoce du Christ dans l'épître aux Hébreux', *Bible et Vie Chrétienne* XXX (1959), 34–44

GALOT J., *La redemption, mystère d'alliance*, Bruges 1965

GAMBLE J., 'Symbol and reality in the Epistle to the Hebrews', *Journal of Biblical Literature* XLV (1926), 162–170

GELIN A., 'La question de "relectures" bibliques à l'intérieur d'une tradition vivante', in *Sacra Pagina. Miscellanea Biblica Congressus Internationalis Catholici de re biblica*, I, Gembloux 1959, 303–315

—— 'Le sacerdoce de l'ancienne alliance', in *La tradition sacerdotale. Etudes sur le sacerdoce*, Le Puy 1959

—— 'Le sacerdoce du Christ d'après l'épître aux Hébreux', in *Etudes sur le sacrement de l'ordre*, Paris 1957, 43–58, with the discussion that followed the paper 59–75

—— 'Messianisme', in *Dictionnaire de la Bible, Supplément* V, cols 1165–1212

GEORGE A., 'Le sacerdoce de la nouvelle alliance', in *La tradition sacerdotale. Etudes sur le sacerdoce*, Le Puy 1959

GIBLET J., 'Le Temple de l'éternelle alliance', *Eglise Vivante* IX (1957), 122–125

GNILKA J., 'Die Erwartung des messianischen Hohenpriesters in den Schriften von Qumran und im Neuen Testament' *Revue de Qumran* II (1960), 395–426

GRAESSER E., 'Der Hebräerbrief 1938–1963', *Theologische Rundschau* XXX (1964), 138–236

GRELOT P., *Le ministère de la nouvelle alliance*, Paris 1967

—— 'Les figures bibliques', *Nouvelle Revue Théologique* LXXXIV (1962), 561–578, 673–698

——'Notre purification par le sang du Christ', *Assemblées du Seigneur*, XXXIV (1963), 64–77

GRELOT P., *Sens chrétien de l'Ancient Testament. Esquisse d'un traité dogmatique*, Paris 1962

GUIGNEBERT C., 'Quelques remarques sur la perfection (*teleiōsis*) et ses voies dans le mystère paulinien', *Revue d'Histoire et de Philosophie Religieuse* VIII (1928), 412–429

GUILLET J., 'Le sacerdoce de la nouvelle alliance', *Christus* II, 5 (1955), 10–28

HAHN, F., *Christologische Hoheitstitel. Ihre Geschichte im frühen Christentum*, Göttingen 1963

HAMP V., 'Melchisedech als Typus', in *Pro Mundi Vita. Festschrift zum eucharistichen Weltkongress*, Munich 1960

HANSON A. T., 'Christ in the Old Testament according to Hebrews', *Studia Evangelica* II (1964), 393–407

HANSON A. T., 'The gospel in the Old Testament according to the Hebrews', *Theology* (1949), 248–252

HANSON, R. P. C., 'The theology of the Epistle to the Hebrews', *Bibliotheca Sacra* CXXI (1964), 323–340

HARVEY J., 'Symbolique et théologie biblique', *Sciences Ecclésiastiques* IX (1957), 147–157

HEIN J., *Jesus the world's perfector. The atonement and the renewal of the world*, London 1959

HÉRING J., 'Eschatologie biblique et idéalisme platonicien' in Davies-Daube, *The background of the New Testament and its eschatology*, Cambridge 1956, 444–463

—— *L'épître aux Hébreux*, Neuchâtel–Paris 1954

HIGGINS A. J. B. (ed), *New Testament essays*, Manchester 1959

HIGGINS A. J. B., 'The Old Testament and some aspects of New Testament Christology', in *Promise and fulfilment*, F. F. Bruce, London 1963

—— 'The priestly Messiah', NTS XIII (1967), 211–239

JEREMIAS J., 'Hebräer 5:7–10', *Zeitschrift für die neutesta-mentliche Wissenschaft* XLIV (1952–1953), 107–111

JONES C. P. M., 'The Epistle to the Hebrews and the Lucan writings', in *Studies in the gospels*, ed D. E. Nineham, Oxford 1955

KÄSEMANN E., *Das wandernde Gottesvolk. Eine Unter-suchung zum Hebräerbrief*, Göttingen 1938

KENNEDY G. T., *St Paul's conception of the priesthood of Melchisedech*, Washington 1951

KISTEMAKER S., *The Psalm citations in the Epistle to the Hebrews*, Amsterdam 1961

KLOKER G., 'Das Hohepriestertum Christi nach dem Hebräer-brief', in *Zeugnis des Geistes: Gabe zum Benedictus-jubiläum 547–1947*, Beuron 1947, 157–169, 299–315

KÖGEL J., *Der Sohn und die Söhne. Eine exegetische Studie zur Hebräer 2:5–18*, Gütersloh 1904

KOSMALA H., *Hebräer-Essener-Christen*, Leiden 1959

KRÄMER H., 'Zu Hebräer 2, vers 10', *Wort und Dienst*, Bethel 1952, 102–107

KÜSS O., 'Der theologische Grundgedanke des Hebräer-briefes'. *Münchener Theologische Zeitschrift* VII (1956), 233–271

LAMPE G. W. H. and WOOLCOMBE K. J., *Essays in Typology*, London 1957

LAMPE G. W. H., 'Hermeneutics and typology', *London Quarterly and Holborn Review* CXC (1965), 17–25

—— 'Typological exegesis', *Theology* LVI (1953), 201–208

LECUYER J., *Le sacerdoce dans le mystère du Christ*, Paris 1957

—— *Le sacrifice de la nouvelle alliance*, Le Puy 1962

—— 'L'oeuvre sacerdotale du Christ', *Vie Spirituelle* CXII (1962), 424–437

LEEMING B., 'Christ the priest', *The Way* V (1965), 3–10

LESÊTRE H., 'Grand prêtre', *Dictionnaire de la Bible* III, col 295–308

—— 'Prêtre', *Dictionnaire de la Bible* V, col 640–662

—— 'Sacrifice', *Dictionnaire de la Bible* V, col 1311–1337

LINDARS B., *New Testament apologetic*, London 1961

LLOYD G. G., 'The Melchizedek order of priesthood in the Epistle to the Hebrews', *Studies in Christian Religion* XXX (1958)

LOANE M. L., *Key texts in the Epistle to the Hebrews*, London 1961

LYONNET S., 'Expiation et intercession; à propos d'une traduction de saint Jérome', *Biblica* XL (1959), 885–901

MACKAY C., 'The order of Melchizedek', *Church Quarterly Review* CXXXVIII (1944), no 276, 175–191

MANSON W., *The Epistle to the Hebrews: An historical and theological reconsideration*, London 1951

MARCHANT G. J. C., 'Sacrifice in the Epistle to the Hebrews', *Evangelical Quarterly* XX (1948), 196ff

MÉDEBIELLE A., 'Expiation'. *Dictionnaire de la Bible*, Supplément 3, 1–262

—— 'Sacrificium expiationis et communionis, Heb 13:20', *Verbum Domini* V (1925), 164–179, 203–220, 238–242

MICHAELIS W., *Skēnē*, TWNT VII, 369–383

MICHEL O., *Der Brief an die Hebräer*, Göttingen 1949

MOE O., 'Das Abendmahl in Hebräerbrief'. *Studia Theologica* IV, 1 (1951), 102–108

—— 'Das irdische und das himmlische Heiligtum. Zur auslegung von Heb 9:4sq', *Theologische Zeitschrift* IX (1953), 23–29

—— 'Das Priestertum Christi im Neuen Testament ausserhalb des Hebräerbriefes', *Theologische Literaturzeitung* LXXII (1947). 235–238

—— 'Der Gedanke des allgemeinen Priestertums in Hebräerbrief', *Theologische Zeitschrift* V (1949), 161–168

MOFFATT J., *The Epistle to the Hebrews*, Edinburgh 1924

MORRIS L., 'Kai Hapax kai dis', *Novum Testamentum* I (1956), 205–208

MOULE C. F. D., 'Sanctuary and sacrifice in the Church of the New Testament', *Journal of Theological Studies*, new series I (1950), 29–41

NAKAGAWA H., *Christology in the Epistle of the Hebrews*, Yale 1955

NOMOTO S., *Die Hohepriester-Typologie im Hebräerbrief. Ihre traditionsgeschictliche Herkunft und ihr religionsgeschichtliche Hintergrund*, Hamburg 1966

OGARA F., 'Christus rex sacerdos secundum ordinem Melchisedech', *Verbum Domini* XIII (1933), 39–51

OMARK R. E., 'The saving of the saviour. Exegesis and Christology in Hebrews', *Interpretation* XII (1958), 39–51

OWEN H. P., 'The "stages of ascent" in Heb 5:11–6:3', NTS III (1957), 243–253

PADOLSKIS V., *L'idée du sacrifice de la croix dans l'épître aux Hébreux*, Vilkaviskis 1935

PENIDO M. T.-L., *Le rôle de l'analogie en théologie dogmatique*, Paris 1931

PEPIN J., *Mythe et allégorie*, Paris 1958

PETUCHOWSKI J. J., 'The controversial figure of Melchizedek', *Hebrew University College Annual* XXVIII (1957), 127ff

PROKSCH O. and KUHN K. G., *Hagios, etc*, TWNT I, 87–117

QUELL G., KITTEL G. and BULTMANN R., *Alētheia etc*, TWNT I, 233–251

RABANOS R., *El sacerdocio de Cristo segun san Pablo*, Madrid 1942

RENDALL R., 'The method of the writer to the Hebrews in using Old Testament quotations', *Evangelical Quarterly* XXVII (1965), 214ff

RIESENFELD H., 'The mythical background of New Testament Christology', in Davies-Daube, *The background of the New Testament and its eschatology*, Cambridge 1956

RIGGENBACH E., 'Der Begriff der *teleiōsis* in Hebräerbrief', *Neue Kirchliche Zeitschrift* (1923), 184–185

RISSI M., 'Die Menschlichkeit Jesu nach Heb 5:7–8', *Theologische Zeitschrift* II (1954), 28–45

ROBINSON W., 'Eschatology of the Epistle to the Hebrews. A study in the christian doctrine of hope', *Encounter* XXII, 1 (1961), 37–51

ROLSON J. W., 'Ta epourania in epistula ad Hebraeos 8:5 et 9:23', *Annales Theologicae-Canonicae* X (1963), 21–44

ROMEO A., 'La spiritualizzazione del culto' and 'Il sacerdozio di Gesù Cristo', in *Enciclopedia del sacerdozio*, ed G. Cacciatore, Florence 1953, 499–529

ROSADINI S., 'De Christi sacerdotio in Epistola ad Hebraeos', *Gregorianum* II (1921), 285–290

ROWELL J. B., 'Our great high priest', *Bibliotheca Sacra* CXVIII (1961), 148–153

RUSCHE H., 'Die Gestalt des Melchisedek', *Münchener Theologische Zeitschrift* VI (1955), 230–252

SABOURIN L., *Redemption sacrificielle. Une enquête exégetique*, Paris 1961

SASSE H., *Aiōn, aiōnios*, TWNT I, 197–209

SAYDON P. P., 'The master idea of the Epistle to the Hebrews', *Mélanges Théologiques* XIII (1961), 19–26

SCHIERSE F. J., *Verheissung und Heilsvollendung. Zur theologischen Grundfrage des Hebräerbriefes*, Munich 1955

SCHILLE G., 'Erwägungen zur Hohepriesterlehre des Hebräerbriefes', *Zeitschrift für die neutestamentliche Wissenschaft* LXIV (1955), 81–109

SCHRENK G., *Hiereus, archiereus*, TWNT III, 257–284

—— *To hieron*, TWNT III, 230–247

SHEEHAN J. F. X., 'Melchisedech in christian consciousness', *Sciences Ecclésiastiques* XVIII (1966), 127–138

SMALLEY S. S., 'The atonement in the Epistle to the Hebrews', *Evangelical Quarterly* XXXIII (1961), 36–43

SNELL A., *New and living way*, London 1959

SOUBIGOU L., *Lumières sur le sacerdoce de Jésus-Christ, prêtre selon l'ordre de Melchisédech*, Paris 1948

SOWERS S. G., *The hermeneutics of Philo and Hebrews*, Zurich 1965 (Basel dissertation)

SPICQ C., 'El sacerdocio de Cristo en la epistola a los Hebreos', *Cultura Biblica* XIII (1956), 232–238

—— 'Hébreux (Epître aux)', in 'Paul', *Dictionnaire de la Bible. Supplément* VII, cols 226–279

—— 'La théologie de l'épître aux Hébreux', *Vie Spirituelle* LXXXVI (1952), 139–153

—— 'La théologie des deux alliances dans l'épître aux Hébreux', *Revue des Sciences Philosophiques et Théologiques* XXXIII (1949), 15–30

—— 'Le philonisme de l'épître aux Hébreux', *Revue Biblique* LVI (1949), 542–572

—— *L'Epître aux Hébreux*. Etudes Bibliques, 2 vols, Paris 1952–53

—— 'L'origine johannique de la conception du Christ prêtre dans l'épître aux Hébreux', in *Aux sources de la tradition chrétienne*, Neuchâtel 1950, 258–269

—— 'Médiation' 4 'Dans le Nouveau Testament', *Dictionnaire de la Bible*, Supplément 5, cols 1020–1083

SQUILLACI D., 'Il sacrificio perpetuo del Messia', *Palestra del Clero* XXXIX (1960), 801–806

STAEHLIN G., *Hapax, ephapax*, TWNT I, 380–383

STOTT W. 'The concept of "offering" in the Epistle to the Hebrews', NTS IX (1962–1963), 62–67

SWETNAM J., 'On the imagery and significance of Heb. 9:9–10', *Catholic Biblical Quarterly* XXVIII (1966), 155–173

—— ' "The greater and more perfect tent." A contribution to the discussion of Heb. 9:11', *Biblica* XLVII (1966), 91–106

SYNGE F. C., *Hebrews and the Scriptures*, London 1959

TASKER R. V. G., *The gospel in the Epistle to the Hebrews*, London 1950

TAYLOR V., *The person of Christ in New Testament teaching*, London 1958

TEODORICO DA CASTEL SAN PIETRO, 'Il sacerdozio celeste di Cristo nella lettera agli Ebrei', *Gregorianum* XXXIX (1958), 319–334

——*L'epistola agli Ebrei*, Turin–Rome 1952

TENNEY M. C., 'A new approach to the book of Hebrews', *Bibliotheca Sacra* CXXIII (1966), 230–236

THOMAS J. T., 'The Old Testament citations in Hebrews', NTS II (1965), 303–325

TORRANCE T. F., *Royal priesthood*, Edinburgh 1955

TRINIDAD J., 'De sacrificio Christi in epistola ad Hebraeos', *Verbum Domini* XIX (1939), 180–186, 207–212

UNGEHAUER J., *Der grosse Priester über dem Hause Gottes. Die Christologie des Hebräerbriefes*, Wurzburg 1939

VAN DER PLOEG J., 'L'exégèse de l'Ancient Testament dans l'épître aux Hébreux', *Revue Biblique* LIV (1947), 187–228

VANHOYE A., 'Christologia a qua initium sumit epistula ad Hebraeos' Heb 1:26, 3, 4, *Verbum Domini* XLIII (1965)

—— 'De "aspectu" oblationis Christi secundum epistulam ad Hebraeos', *Verbum Domini* XXXVII (1959), 32–38

—— 'De instauratione novae dispensationis' Heb 9:15–23, *Verbum Domini* XLIV (1966), 113–130

—— 'De sessione coelesti in epistula ad Hebraeos', *Verbum Domini* XLIV (1966), 131–134

—— 'Expiation ancienne et sacrifice du Christ', *Assemblées du Seigneur* LXXII (1964), 18–35

—— 'Jesus "fidelis ei qui fecit eum"' Heb 3:2, *Verbum Domini* XLV (1967), 291–305

—— 'La structure centrale de l'épître aux Hébreux' Heb. 8:1–9:28, *Recherches de Science Religieuse* XLVII (1959), 44–60

—— *La structure littéraire de l'épître aux Hébreux*. Studia Neotestamentica, Studia I, Paris-Bruges 1963

—— 'Le parfait grand-prêtre' Heb 7:23–27, *Assemblées du Seigneur* XCIII (1965), 15–31

—— '*L'oikoumené* dans l'épître aux Hébreux', *Biblica* XLV (1964), 248–253

—— 'Mundatio per sanguinem' Heb 9:22–32, *Verbum Domini* XLIV (1966), 177–191

—— 'Par la tente plus grande et plus parfaite ...' Heb. 9:11, *Biblica* XLVI (1965)

—— 'Structure littéraire et thèmes théologiques de l'épître aux Hébreux', *Analecta Biblica* XVIII (1963), 175–181

VAWTER B., 'The fuller sense, some considerations', *Catholic Biblical Quarterly* XXVI (1964), 85–96

VITTI A. M., 'Didicit oboedientiam', *Verbum Domini* XII (1932), 264–272

—— 'Exauditus pro sua reverentia', *Verbum Domini* XIV (1934), 86–92, 108–114

—— 'La dottrina di San Paolo sul sacerdozio', *Rivista Biblica Italiana* IV (1957), 1–16

—— 'Ultimi studi sulla lettera agli Ebrei', *Biblica* XXI (1941), 412–432

VON RAD G., *Old Testament Theology*, 2 vols, Eng edn, London 1965

Vos G., *The teaching of the Epistle to the Hebrews*, Grand Rapids 1956

WENSCHKEWITZ H., 'Die Spiritualisierung der Kultusbegriffe Tempel, Priester und Opfer im Neuen Testament', *Angelos* IV, 4 (1932), 71–230

WESTCOTT B. F., *The Epistle to the Hebrews*, 3rd edn repr, London 1914

WESTERMANN C. (ed), *Essays on Old Testament interpretation*, Eng edn, London 1963

WIKGREN A., 'Patterns of perfection in the Epistle to the Hebrews', NTS VI (1960), 159–167

WILLIAMS R. R., *Reading through Hebrews*, London 1960

WILLIAMSON R., 'Platonism and Hebrews', *Scottish Journal of Theology* XVI (1963), 415–424

WINTER A., *Hapax, ephapax in Hebräerbrief. Eine exegetisch-bibeltheologische Studie zur Theologie der Einmaligkeit*, Rome 1960 (Gregorian dissertation)

WOLFZORN E. E., 'Realized eschatology. An exposition of Charles H. Dodd's thesis', *Ephemerides Theologiae Lovanienses* LXXIII (1962), 44–70

WORDEN T., 'Before reading the Epistle to the Hebrews', *Scripture* XIV (1962), 48–57

WUEST K. S., 'Hebrews six in the Greek New Testament', *Bibliotheca Sacra* CXIX (1962), 45–53

YADIN Y., 'The scrolls and the Epistle to the Hebrews', in *Aspects of the Dead Sea Scrolls*, Scripta Hierosolymitana IV (1957) 36–45

ZIMMERMANN H., *Die Hohepriester-Christologie des Hebräerbriefes*, Paderborn 1964

Index of authors cited

Index
of biblical references

Old Testament

214